The Fundamentals of Hebrew Accents

This book is designed to serve as a textbook for intermediate Hebrew students and above. Sung Jin Park presents the fundamental features of the Tiberian Hebrew accents, focusing on their divisions and exegetical roles. Providing innovative methods for diagramming biblical texts, the volume explores the two major rules (hierarchy and dichotomy) of disjunctive accents. Students will also attain biblical insights from the exegetical application of the biblical texts that Hebrew syntax alone does not provide. Park's volume shows how the new perspectives on Hebrew accents enhance our understanding of biblical texts.

Sung Jin Park is Associate Professor of Biblical Studies and Dean of Asian Studies at Midwestern Baptist Theological Seminary. He is the author of *Typology in Biblical Hebrew Meter: A Generative Metrical Approach* (2017) and numerous academic articles.

The Fundamentals of Hebrew Accents

Divisions and Exegetical Roles Beyond Syntax

SUNG JIN PARK
Midwestern Baptist Theological Seminary

CAMBRIDGE
UNIVERSITY PRESS

University Printing House, Cambridge CB2 8BS, United Kingdom

One Liberty Plaza, 20th Floor, New York, NY 10006, USA

477 Williamstown Road, Port Melbourne, VIC 3207, Australia

314–321, 3rd Floor, Plot 3, Splendor Forum, Jasola District Centre,
New Delhi – 110025, India

79 Anson Road, #06–04/06, Singapore 079906

Cambridge University Press is part of the University of Cambridge.

It furthers the University's mission by disseminating knowledge in the pursuit of
education, learning, and research at the highest international levels of excellence.

www.cambridge.org
Information on this title: www.cambridge.org/9781108479936
DOI: 10.1017/9781108801782

© Cambridge University Press 2020

This publication is in copyright. Subject to statutory exception
and to the provisions of relevant collective licensing agreements,
no reproduction of any part may take place without the written
permission of Cambridge University Press.

First published 2020

Printed in the United Kingdom by TJ International Ltd, Padstow Cornwall

A catalogue record for this publication is available from the British Library.

ISBN 978-1-108-47993-6 Hardback
ISBN 978-1-108-79098-7 Paperback

Cambridge University Press has no responsibility for the persistence or accuracy of
URLs for external or third-party internet websites referred to in this publication
and does not guarantee that any content on such websites is, or will remain,
accurate or appropriate.

In loving memory of my late professor, David B. Weisberg, who introduced me to the wonderful world of the Masorah

Contents

List of Tables		*page* ix
Preface		xi
List of Abbreviations		xv
1	INTRODUCTION TO TIBERIAN HEBREW ACCENTS	1
	1.1 The Tiberian Hebrew Accents	1
	1.2 Discussion of Accentual Positions	5
	1.3 Summary	7
	1.4 Exercises	8
2	MAJOR RULES OF HEBREW ACCENTS	10
	2.1 The Hierarchy Rule of Disjunctive Accents	10
	2.2 The Dichotomy Rule of Disjunctive Accents	14
	2.3 Summary	20
	2.4 Exercises	20
3	SUBSTITUTIONS OF DISJUNCTIVE ACCENTS (I)	23
	3.1 Disjunctives at the D0 Level	23
	3.2 Disjunctives at the D1 Level	25
	3.3 Summary	33
	3.4 Exercises	34
4	SUBSTITUTIONS OF DISJUNCTIVE ACCENTS (II)	35
	4.1 Disjunctives at the D2 Level	35
	4.2 Disjunctives at the D3 Level	42
	4.3 Summary	49
	4.4 Exercises	50

vii

viii   *Contents*

5 CONJUNCTIVE ACCENTS   53
     5.1 Preference of Conjunctive Accents   53
     5.2 Examples for the Preference of Conjunctive
          Accents   55
     5.3 Secondary Accents   64
     5.4 Summary   69
     5.5 Exercises   69

6 MINOR RULES OF HEBREW ACCENTS   73
     6.1 The Simplification and Division Rules   73
     6.2 The Spirantization (*Sandhi*) Rule   85
     6.3 The *Nesiga* Rule   85
     6.4 Summary   88
     6.5 Exercises   89

7 THE DIVISIONS BY HEBREW ACCENTS   93
     7.1 Linguistic Representation of the Accentual
          Divisions   93
     7.2 Prosodic Representation of the Divisions   103
     7.3 Performance Structure   112
     7.4 Summary   115

8 THE EXEGETICAL ROLES OF THE DIVISIONS   116
     8.1 Clarifying Ambiguous Meanings   116
     8.2 Emphasizing Certain Words or Phrases   120
     8.3 Creating Dramatic Effect in Biblical
          Narrative   125
     8.4 Summary   131

Appendix A The Functional Development of the Tiberian Hebrew
*   Accents*   133
Appendix B Three Accentuation Systems within the Masoretic
*   Tradition*   143
Appendix C The Accents of the "Three Books" in the Tiberian
*   Tradition*   149
Appendix D The Functions of Paseq *and* Maqqeph   157

Bibliography   165
Subject Index   171
Scripture Index   175

Tables

1	Disjunctive accents in the Twenty-One Books	*page* 3
2	Conjunctive accents in the Twenty-One Books	4
3	Hierarchy among the disjunctive accents	12
4	Substitute disjunctives for regular disjunctives	13
5	Hierarchical level of disjunctive accents	15
6	List of final disjunctives	19
7	Summary of substitutions of disjunctives	49
8	Preference of conjunctives	54
9	Comparison between syntactic and prosodic hierarchies	105
10	Comparison between modern and Tiberian hierarchies	108
11	The prosodic hierarchy of Isaiah 1:10	111
12	Examples of performance structure	114
13	Babylonian accents and their Tiberian equivalents	146
14	Disjunctive accents in the Three Books	150
15	Conjunctive accents in the Three Books	150
16	Hierarchy among the disjunctives in the Three Books	151
17	Substitute disjunctives for regular disjunctives in the Three Books	151
18	Preference of conjunctives in the Three Books	152

Preface

As the title indicates, this volume presents the fundamental features of the Tiberian Hebrew accents, focusing especially on their divisions and exegetical roles. My attention was first drawn to the Tiberian accentuation system during the period of my doctoral study at Hebrew Union College–Jewish Institute of Religion. My late professor, David B. Weisberg, to whom I dedicate this book, opened my eyes to the wonderland of the Masorah. Due to its intricacies, there are still unsearched areas in this field; the masoretic accentuation systems remain largely unexplored, especially when compared with other linguistic features, such as grammar, syntax, and semantics. As an introductory guide to Tiberian Hebrew accents, I hope this book opens a door for many Hebrew students to the world of masoretic studies.

As a preface, I would like to make several comments about the limits and scope of this volume:

1. This volume is designed to serve as a textbook for intermediate Hebrew students and above. The best place to use this book is between learning the Biblical Hebrew syntax and learning textual criticism. Once students learn the syntax of Biblical Hebrew, they are ready to use *Biblia Hebraica Stuttgartensia* (*BHS*) based on the Tiberian Hebrew tradition. Students will appreciate learning about the Hebrew accents before they explore text-critical issues. This volume uses *BHS* as a main text for discussions and examples.

xi

xii

2. This book deals with the Tiberian Hebrew accents. There are three masoretic traditions: Babylonian, Palestinian, and Tiberian. Each tradition carries different graphemes for the vowel and accent signs. The Tiberian system represents the latest development among the masoretic traditions because of its full-fledged systematic structure of vocalization and accentuation. For discussion of the Babylonian and Palestinian accentuation systems, please refer to Appendix B.

3. There are two accentuation systems in the Tiberian manuscripts of the Hebrew Bible: one used in the "Three Books" (Psalms, Proverbs, and Job [except for the narrative portion of Job 1:1–3:1 and 42:7–17]) and the other in all the remaining material (the so-called Twenty-One Books). This book considers only the latter, which represents a more developed and improved system than the former, although both systems are functionally the same. On the accents in the "Three Books," see Appendix C.

4. Although the issues of pausal forms are deeply associated with Hebrew accents, this book will not deal with them in detail. Rather, it mainly concerns Hebrew accents and their divisions and exegetical roles.

5. The book has eight chapters. Hebrew professors may wish to teach through this book for eight weeks, covering one chapter a week. Some chapters include exercises to help students reinforce what they have learned.

6. I refer to several major works throughout this book. These works are as follows:

Mordecai Breuer, פיסוק טעמים שבמקרא: תורת דקדוק הטעמים (Jerusalem: Hahistadrut Hatzionit, 1958) and טעמי המקרא בכ"א ספרים ובספרי אמ"ת (Jerusalem: Mikhlalah, 1982);

Miles B. Cohen, *The System of Accentuation in the Hebrew Bible* (Minneapolis, MN: Milco Press, 1969);

Bezalel E. Dresher, "The Prosodic Basis of the Tiberian Hebrew System of Accents," *Language* 70 (1994): 1–52;

Preface xiii

Joshua R. Jacobson, *Chanting the Hebrew Bible: The Art of Cantillation* (2nd & expanded edn., Philadelphia: Jewish Publication Society, 2017);

James D. Price, *The Syntax of Masoretic Accents in the Hebrew Bible.* SBEC 27. (Lewiston, NY: Edwin Mellen Press, 1990);

David B. Weisberg, "The Rare Accents of the Twenty-One Books," *Jewish Quarterly Review* 56, no. 4 (1966): 314–336; 57, no. 1 (1967): 57–70; and 57, no. 3 (1967): 227–238;

William Wickes, *A Treatise on the Accentuation of the Twenty-One So-Called Prose Books of the Old Testament* (London: Oxford University Press, 1887); and

Israel Yeivin, *Introduction to the Tiberian Masorah* (E. J. Revell, trans. & ed., Missoula, MT: Scholars' Press, 1980).

There are numerous people to whom I owe a great debt of gratitude during the preparation of this volume. In particular, I have benefited from interactions with several scholars who have offered comments and assistance: James D. Price (Temple Baptist Seminary), Aron Dotan (Tel Aviv University), David Marcus (The Jewish Theological Seminary), Alan F. Cooper (The Jewish Theological Seminary), and Eugene H. Merrill (Dallas Theological Seminary).

I also wish to thank the administration and library staff of Midwestern Baptist Theological Seminary for their support and encouragement, as well as Ben Noonan and Eileen Park for their incredible editorial efforts. I would like to offer my special thanks to the editors of *Hebrew Studies, Sefarad, Cognitive Psychology,* MIT Press, Gorgias Press, Edwin Mellen Press, Brill, and Chorev Publishing House for permissions to use portions of their published materials for this study. I thank Beatrice Rehl and Eilidh Burrett at Cambridge University Press for their support of this book's production. Most of all, I would like to express my special gratitude to my wife, Alice, for her enduring love and support.

Abbreviations

ABD	*The Anchor Bible Dictionary*. Edited by D. N. Freedman. 6 vols. New York: Doubleday, 1992.
BHS	*Biblia Hebraica Stuttgartensia*
BJRL	*Bulletin of the John Rylands University Library of Manchester*
EncJud	*Encyclopaedia Judaica*. Edited by Fred Skolnik. 22 vols. Detroit, MI: Macmillan Reference USA, and Jerusalem: Keter Publishing House, 2007.
HS	*Hebrew Studies*
IOMS	International Organization for Masoretic Studies
JANES	*Journal of the Ancient Near Eastern Society*
JQR	*Jewish Quarterly Review*
JSJ	*Journal for the Study of Judaism*
JSS	*Journal of Semitic Studies*
MAS	The Masoretic accentuation system
MT	The Masoretic Text
ODL	Outstanding Dissertation in Linguistics Series
PLO	Porta Linguarum Orientalium
SBEC	Studies in the Bible and Early Christianity
SBLMS	Society of Biblical Literature Masoretic Studies
SGG	Studies in Generative Grammar
VT	*Vetus Testamentum*

1 Introduction to Tiberian Hebrew Accents

As we begin our exploration of the Hebrew accent, it is necessary to lay a foundation for understanding the masoretic accentuation system. Thus, in this first chapter we will present a brief overview of the masoretic traditions and introduce two kinds of Hebrew accents found in the Twenty-One Books: disjunctive and conjunctive accents. We will also discuss the 28 Hebrew accents' names and their accentual positions.

1.1 The Tiberian Hebrew Accents

In transmitting the ancient legacy of the Hebrew Bible, the Masoretes developed a written system for the vocalic tradition that had been orally transmitted throughout the centuries. They were truly guardians of the Hebrew language tradition[1] rather than innovators.[2] Goshen-Gottstein asserts, "The work of the Masoretes, which reached a peak in the Aleppo Codex, is to be understood as the invention and perfection of an ever more refined graphic notation for an age-old oral tradition which endeavored to note down with the greatest possible

---

[1] Barr, *Comparative Philology and the Text of the Old Testament*, 194–222; Kutcher, "Contemporary Studies in Northwestern Semitic," 21–51.
[2] Kahle, *The Cairo Geniza*, 164–186.

2   *Introduction to Tiberian Hebrew Accents*

exactness, the smallest details of the customary liturgical way of reading the Bible."[3]

There are three masoretic traditions: Babylonian, Palestinian, and Tiberian. Each tradition uses different graphemes for the vowel and accent signs. The Babylonian and Palestinian traditions were eventually supplanted by the Tiberian system, considered the best tradition because its system of vocalization and accentuation is the most comprehensive and sophisticated of the three.

The Tiberian tradition adds the following components to the traditional consonantal text: (1) a particular layout of the text and codicological form of the manuscripts; (2) indications of divisions of paragraphs (known in Hebrew as *pisqa'ot* or *parashiyyot*); (3) accent signs; (4) vowels; (5) notes on the text, written in the margins of the manuscript; and (6) masoretic treatises at the end of the text.[4] The accents in the Tiberian tradition are the subject explored in this book.

There are two kinds of Hebrew accents in the Twenty-One Books: disjunctive accents and conjunctive accents. Disjunctive accents indicate stresses as well as phrasal divisions ranging "from full stop to various shades of shorter pauses."[5] Hence, disjunctives function as separators. However, disjunctives do not suffice to indicate all word stresses because any word without a disjunctive accent may also bear word stress. For this reason, an additional accent type is necessary. This other type of accent, called a conjunctive, normally functions to connect two disjunctives. Conjunctives were not originally considered accents, but they later came to be treated as one kind of accent because they bear relatively weak stresses as connectors between dominant disjunctive accents.

---

[3] Goshen-Gottstein, "The Rise of the Tiberian Bible Text," 93. Harry Orlinsky comments, "All the Masoretes, from first to last, were essentially preservers and recorders of the pronunciation of Hebrew as they heard it." See also Ginsburg, *Introduction to the Massoretico-Critical Edition of the Hebrew Bible*, xxxii.

[4] Khan, *A Short Introduction to the Tiberian Masoretic Bible and Its Reading Tradition*, 3.

[5] Waltke and O'Connor, *An Introduction to Biblical Hebrew Syntax*, 29.

1.1 The Tiberian Hebrew Accents

The functions of disjunctive and conjunctive accents will be discussed in detail in Chapters 2–6. Here, I simply list the names of the accents in the Twenty-One Books and describe their marking positions (see Tables 1–2).

1.1.1 *Disjunctive Accents*

Table 1 *Disjunctive accents in the Twenty-One Books*

Name	Accent position	Remarks	Meaning
Soph Pasuq	דָּבָר׃	At the end of a whole verse	"end of a verse"
Silluq	דָּבָר	–	"separation"
Athnach	דָּבָר	–	"cause to rest"
Segolta	דָּבָר֒	Postpositive	"cluster"
Shalsheleth	דָּבָר׀	–	"triplet"
Little Zaqeph	דָּבָר	–	"small upright"
Great Zaqeph	דָּבָר	–	"big upright"
Rebia	דָּבָר	–	"resting"
Tiphcha	דָּבָר	–	"disturbance"
Zarqa	דָּבָר֮	Postpositive	"scattering"
Pashta	מֶלֶךְ֙	Postpositive	"extending"
Yethib	דָּבָר	Prepositive	"resting"
Tebir	דָּבָר	–	"broken"
Geresh	דָּבָר	–	"expulsion"
Garshaim	דָּבָר	–	"double expulsion"
Pazer	דָּבָר	–	"scattering"
Great Pazer (or *Qarne Para*)	דָּבָר	–	"big scattering"
Great Telisha	דָּבָר	Prepositive	"big drawing out"
Legarmeh	דָּבָר׀	–	"break"

1.1.2 Conjunctive Accents

Table 2 *Conjunctive accents in the Twenty-One Books*

Name	Accent position	Remarks	Meaning
Munach	דְּבָר	–	"sustained"
Mahpak	דְּבָר	–	"inverted"
Mereka	דְּבָר	–	"prolonged"
Double Mereka	דְּבָר	–	"doubly prolonged"
Darga	דְּבָר	–	"stopping"
Azla (or *Qadma*)	דְּבָר	–	"proceeding"
Little Telisha	דְּבָר	Postpositive	"small drawing out"
Galgal	דְּבָר	–	"rolling over"
Mayela	וַיֵּצֵא־נֹחַ	Only before *Athnach* or *Silluq*	"inclined"

The following accents appear in Exodus 1:1.

וְאֵ֗לֶּה שְׁמוֹת֙ בְּנֵ֣י יִשְׂרָאֵ֔ל הַבָּאִ֖ים מִצְרָ֑יְמָה

Little Zaqeph   *Pashta*   *Rebia*

Athnach   *Tiphcha*   *Munach*

אֵ֣ת יַעֲקֹ֔ב אִ֥ישׁ וּבֵית֖וֹ בָּֽאוּ׃

Little Zaqeph

Soph Pasuq →

Silluq   *Tiphcha*   *Mereka*   *Munach*

Because of the variety of Tiberian Hebrew accents, it can be difficult to remember them all, but it is important to memorize at least the following accents that appear most often: the disjunctive accents *Soph Pasuq, Silluq,*

1.2 Discussion of Accentual Positions

Athnach, Tiphcha, Little Zaqeph, Segolta, Tebir, Pashta, Zarqa, Rebia, Geresh; and the conjunctive accents *Munach, Mahpak,* and *Mereka.*

1.2 Discussion of Accentual Positions

Having listed the disjunctive and conjunctive accents, we turn now to several notable characteristics of their positions:

(1) *Soph Pasuq* has not traditionally been considered one of the disjunctive accents because it does not mark the stressed syllable of any word. Instead, at the end of a verse, it functions as a marker to distinguish the current verse from the next verse. Thus, its function as a separator is identical with that of other disjunctive accents, and it always occurs with *Silluq.* For this reason, this book treats *Soph Pasuq* as one of the disjunctives.

(2) Hebrew accents can have three major positions:

   a. Most accents are placed in normal position, in other words, over or under the stressed syllable of a word.

   b. The three accents (*Segolta, Zarqa,* and *Little Telisha*) are placed over the second half of the final letter of a word. They are the so-called postpositive accents. *Pashta* is also postpositive, but its positioning differs slightly from the other postpositive accents, and it must be distinguished from *Azla* because both accents' signs are identical.[6]

     (i) When the last syllable of a word is stressed, and when that syllable is closed (CVC type), *Azla* is located over the stressed syllable, while *Pashta* is over the second half of the last letter.

---

[6] Cohen, *The System of Accentuation in the Hebrew Bible,* 8–9.

Azla	Pashta
דָּבָ֨ר	דָּבָ֙ר

(ii) When the last syllable of a word is stressed, and when that syllable is open (CV type), *Azla* is located over the last letter, while *Pashta* is over the second half of the last letter.

Azla	Pashta
עַבְדְּ֨ךָ	עַבְדְּ֙ךָ

(iii) When the last syllable of a word is not stressed, *Azla* appears over the stressed syllable. However, unlike other postpositive accents, two *Pashta*s are used: one over the second half of the stressed syllable, and another over the second half of the last letter. Although two *Pashta*s are used, only the second *Pashta* (the one over the second half of the final letter) counts. The first *Pashta* is just a marker to indicate the stressed syllable.

Azla	Two *Pashta*s
מֶ֨לֶךְ	מֶ֙לֶ֙ךְ

c. There are two prepositive accents: *Yethib* (under the first letter of a word) and *Great Telisha* (over the first letter of a word). The signs of *Yethib* and *Mahpak* are identical, but *Mahpak* appears under the stressed syllable, immediately following the vowel sign, whereas *Yethib* is always placed in front of the vowel sign of the first letter.

דְּבָ֤ר	דְּ֚בָר
Mahpak	Yethib

(3) There are two accents appearing together with *Paseq* (a vertical stroke): *Shalsheleth* and *Legarmeh*. In the Three Books (the so-called poetic books), *Shalsheleth* appears

1.3 Summary

either as a conjunctive or as a disjunctive accent depending on the presence of *Paseq*. *Shalsheleth* with *Paseq* is a disjunctive accent, but *Shalsheleth* without *Paseq* serves as a conjunctive accent. The shape of *Legarmeh* looks exactly like a combination of *Munach* and *Paseq*. Appendix D explains in detail how to distinguish between *Legarmeh* and a combination of *Munach* and *Paseq*.

נָחָשׁ | שָׂרָף (Deuteronomy 8:15)

Paseq

אֶת־כָּל־הַיְקוּם | אֲשֶׁר | (Gen. 7:23)

Legarmeh   *Legarmeh*

(4) *Mayela* is not a true conjunctive accent, but a secondary accent like *Metheg* (identical with *Silluq* in shape). As a secondary accent, *Mayela* only appears in the same word stressed by *Athnach* or *Silluq*. Because the shapes of *Mayela* and *Tiphcha* are identical, W. Wickes suggests that *Mayela* is indeed *Tiphcha* as a secondary accent.[7] *Mayela* appears where *Metheg* would be expected. For example, Leviticus 21:4 has:

לֹא יִטַּמָּא בַּעַל בְּעַמָּיו לְהֵחַלּוֹ:

Silluq

Mayela

1.3 Summary

In this chapter, we explored several items that lay the foundation for understanding Hebrew accents. We surveyed

---

[7] Wickes, *A Treatise on the Accentuation of the Twenty-One*, 73.

8   *Introduction to Tiberian Hebrew Accents*

the three masoretic traditions and presented the disjunctive
and conjunctive accents in the Twenty-One Books. We also
discussed the 28 Hebrew accents' names and their accentual
positions. This provides us a basis for examining the functions
and specific characteristics of the accents, topics that will be
covered in the next several chapters.

1.4 Exercises

For each provided Bible verse, circle the accents, write their
names, and identify whether they are disjunctive or conjunctive.

(1) Genesis 1:1

בְּרֵאשִׁית בָּרָא אֱלֹהִים אֵת הַשָּׁמַיִם וְאֵת
הָאָרֶץ׃

(2) 1 Samuel 2:1

וַתִּתְפַּלֵּל חַנָּה וַתֹּאמַר עָלַץ לִבִּי בַּיהֹוָה
רָמָה קַרְנִי בַּיהֹוָה רָחַב פִּי עַל־אוֹיְבַי כִּי
שָׂמַחְתִּי בִּישׁוּעָתֶךָ׃

(3) Deuteronomy 1:1

אֵלֶּה הַדְּבָרִים אֲשֶׁר דִּבֶּר מֹשֶׁה אֶל־כָּל־
יִשְׂרָאֵל בְּעֵבֶר הַיַּרְדֵּן בַּמִּדְבָּר בָּעֲרָבָה מוֹל
סוּף בֵּין־פָּארָן וּבֵין־תֹּפֶל וְלָבָן וַחֲצֵרֹת וְדִי
זָהָב׃

1.4 Exercises 9

(4) Genesis 2:1-4

וַיְכֻלּוּ הַשָּׁמַיִם וְהָאָרֶץ וְכָל־צְבָאָם:

וַיְכַל אֱלֹהִים בַּיּוֹם הַשְּׁבִיעִי מְלַאכְתּוֹ אֲשֶׁר
עָשָׂה וַיִּשְׁבֹּת בַּיּוֹם הַשְּׁבִיעִי מִכָּל־מְלַאכְתּוֹ
אֲשֶׁר עָשָׂה:

וַיְבָרֶךְ אֱלֹהִים אֶת־יוֹם הַשְּׁבִיעִי וַיְקַדֵּשׁ אֹתוֹ
כִּי בוֹ שָׁבַת מִכָּל־מְלַאכְתּוֹ אֲשֶׁר־בָּרָא
אֱלֹהִים לַעֲשׂוֹת:

2 Major Rules of Hebrew Accents

Having laid a foundation for understanding the masoretic accentuation system in the preceding chapter, we now explore the major rules that govern the function of the disjunctive accents. Most Hebrew verses, both prose and poetic, consist of two main parts that are called "hemistichs." Thus, Hebrew verses have a "parallelistic structure" with each parallel element set apart by a disjunctive accent. The hierarchy and dichotomy rules are essential to understanding the major divisions of the disjunctive accents. In this chapter, we will examine these two rules and also learn the process for diagramming the accentuation of a Hebrew verse.

2.1 The Hierarchy Rule of Disjunctive Accents

The first rule of Hebrew accents is that they follow a hierarchy that begins with a distinction between disjunctives and conjunctives. As mentioned in Chapter 1, disjunctive accents function as separators in the hierarchical order, whereas conjunctives – which have no hierarchical arrangement – serve as connectors between disjunctive accents. The disjunctive force of a disjunctive accent is relative to the context, but the hierarchical order among the disjunctive accents is almost absolute within a verse.

2.1 The Hierarchy Rule of Disjunctive Accents   11

Some older scholars such as Samuel Lee described the hierarchical arrangement of the disjunctive accents with the names of political ranks:[1]

Emperors: *Silluq, Athnach*
Kings: *Segolta, Little Zaqeph, Great Zaqeph, Tiphcha, Rebia*
Dukes: *Zarqa, Pashta, Tebir, Geresh, Garshaim*
Counts: *Pazer, Great Telisha*
Servants: all the conjunctive accents

Within this system, the higher the rank of a given disjunctive accent, the larger domain it governs in a sentence. Furthermore, the domain that a higher disjunctive accent governs may consist of several smaller domains governed by other lesser disjunctive accents subordinate to their higher disjunctive accent. For example, *Athnach* and *Silluq* are emperors. That means that *Athnach* and *Silluq* govern the first and the second halves of a Hebrew verse, respectively. In the first half of a Hebrew verse ruled by *Athnach*, there may be two smaller parts ruled by *Tiphcha* and *Little Zaqeph*, respectively.

Recently, James D. Price has proposed a more precise and detailed understanding of the disjunctive accents' hierarchy based on their syntactic functions.[2] I adopt his hierarchy in this book because it best explains the function of the disjunctive accents.

Several explanations about Table 3 are in order:

(1) A disjunctive accent governs a specific domain in a verse. Each disjunctive accent is located at the end of that domain, and its domain extends toward the beginning of the verse until it meets an accent of equal or higher rank.

(2) As explained in Chapter 1, *Soph Pasuq* is treated as a disjunctive accent. Furthermore, because *Soph Pasuq* governs a whole verse, it is the highest in rank.

---

[1] Lee, *A Grammar of the Hebrew Language*, 378–381.
[2] Price, *The Syntax of Masoretic Accents in the Hebrew Bible*, 29–30.

12   *Major Rules of Hebrew Accents*

Table 3 *Hierarchy among the disjunctive accents*

| Hierarchy | Disjunctive accents | Defined subordinates | |
		Near	Remote
I	*Soph Pasuq*	*Silluq*	*Athnach*
II	*Silluq*	*Tiphcha*	*Little Zaqeph*
	Athnach	*Tiphcha*	*Little Zaqeph*
III	*Tiphcha*	*Tebir*	*Rebia*
	Little Zaqeph	*Pashta*	*Rebia*
	Segolta	*Zarqa*	*Rebia*
IV	*Tebir*	*Geresh*	*Pazer/ Great Telisha*
	Pashta	*Geresh*	*Pazer/ Great Telisha*
	Zarqa	*Geresh*	*Pazer/ Great Telisha*
	Rebia	*Geresh*	*Pazer/ Great Telisha*
V	*Geresh*		Empty
	Pazer		Empty
	Great Telisha		Empty

(3) In Hierarchy V, the word "Empty" means there exists only one word or a one-word unit left with either *Geresh, Pazer,* or *Great Telisha* without any subordinate disjunctives.[3]

(4) One may wonder why some disjunctive accents such as *Shalsheleth, Great Zaqeph, Yethib, Garshaim,* and *Great Pazer* are not included in Table 3. The reason for their omission is that these rare accents were added later for medieval Jewish cantillation purposes (i.e., to mark certain melodic tones and to clarify the interpretation of certain verses in the haggadic tradition).[4] Thus, these accents function as substitute disjunctives for regular disjunctives under certain phonological conditions such as the

---

[3] Price, *The Syntax of Masoretic Accents in the Hebrew Bible,* 29.

[4] Weisberg, "The Rare Accents of the Twenty-One Books," 227–238. The Tiberian accentuation system was not established at one time; rather, as discussed in Appendix A, it developed in several stages over a period of time.

2.1 The Hierarchy Rule of Disjunctive Accents

Table 4 *Substitute disjunctives for regular disjunctives*

Regular disjunctives	Substitute disjunctives
Little Zaqeph	Great Zaqeph
Little Zaqeph	Segolta
Segolta	Shalsheleth
Pashta	Yethib
Rebia	Pashta
Geresh	Garshaim
Pazer	Great Pazer
Pazer	Great Telisha

domain of regular disjunctives being empty (i.e., one word or word-unit). The accent each substitutes for is outlined in Table 4. Chapters 3–4 discuss these substitute accents in more detail.

Having explained Price's hierarchy, let us now apply it to a specific verse from the Hebrew Bible. Consider, for example, Exodus 1:9:

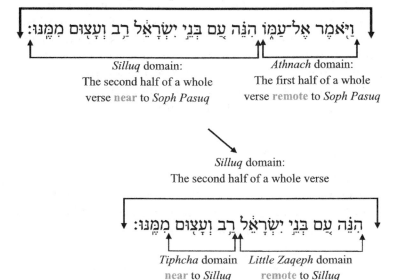

14   *Major Rules of Hebrew Accents*

2.2 The Dichotomy Rule of Disjunctive Accents

Within the hierarchical arrangement of the disjunctive accents, the second rule for accents – the dichotomy rule – applies. The dichotomy rule states that a domain governed by a disjunctive accent is divided by other disjunctive accents of a grade below in a dichotomic way, in other words, as a binary branching system (compare parallelism in biblical Hebrew poetry). Miles Cohen states:

> The basic principle of logical division which is apparent from even a superficial examination can be called the dichotomy of the verse, that is, the division of a verse into two parts. By repeated application of the process of dichotomous division, the two separate parts of the verse are themselves divided into two smaller parts, those minor subdivisions further divided, and so on, until that part is reached where a subdivision consists of *only two words (called a simple phrase) or of only a single word*. At this point the phrase is no longer subject to division, and the process of continuous dichotomy ceases.[5]

In light of the dichotomy rule, it is helpful to think of the disjunctive accents in terms of four different levels ranging from D0 to D3 (see Table 5). The level 0 accent indicates the strongest major break found in the verse, whereas the level 3 accent indicates the weakest. *Soph Pasuq* is excluded from this system because it governs a whole verse and makes a separation from the next verse, not within a verse.

In any discrete phrase marked by disjunctive accent Di, a D_{i+1} accent further divides that phrase.

2.2.1 *Diagramming verses*

The best way to represent the dichotomy rule is through diagramming. Building on the work of Mordecai Breuer, Cohen developed his own diagramming method, which has become the easiest and most convenient way to depict

---

[5] Cohen, *The System of Accentuation in the Hebrew Bible*, 12. (italics mine).

2.2 The Dichotomy Rule of Disjunctive Accents   15

Table 5 *Hierarchical level of disjunctive accents*

Level	Disjunctive accents
D0	*Silluq*
	Athnach
D1	*Tiphcha*
	Little Zaqeph
	Segolta
D2	*Tebir*
	Pashta
	Zarqa
	Rebia
D3	*Geresh*
	Pazer
	Great Telisha

the dichotomy rule.[6] I will adopt Cohen's system in this book.

A verse can be diagrammed using three simple steps:

(1) Determine all the disjunctive accents in a verse.
(2) Group the disjunctive accents according to their hierarchical level from D0 to D3.
(3) Draw a dividing line for each domain. The height and thickness of the line should show the relative strength of the division marked by that line, and the length of the line should represent the domain governed by the disjunctive accent over the final word to the right of that line. A conjunctive accent should be represented by the symbol C.

Let us apply these steps to a specific verse, Isaiah 5:1, as an example. Doing so yields the following:

---

[6] Cohen, *The System of Accentuation in the Hebrew Bible*, 35–42; Breuer, פיסוק טעמים שבמקרא: תורת דקדוק הטעמים, 1–8.

(1) Determine all the disjunctive accents in a given verse. There are four disjunctive accents in Isaiah 5:1a: *Athnach, Tiphcha, Little Zaqeph,* and *Pashta* and three disjunctive accents in Isaiah 5:1b: *Silluq, Tiphcha,* and *Tebir.*
(2) Group the disjunctive accents according to their hierarchical level from D0 to D3.
> In Isaiah 5:1a:
> D0: *Athnach*
> D1: *Tiphcha, Little Zaqeph*
> D2: *Pashta*
>
> In Isaiah 5:1b:
> D0: *Silluq*
> D1: *Tiphcha*
> D2: *Tebir*
(3) Draw a dividing line for each domain.

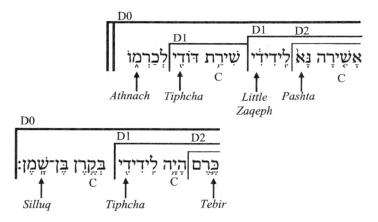

As indicated by this example, a verse's major dichotomy should be marked by a double-thick line. When more than one accent at the D_{i+1} level appears under the Di level, the dividing lines of the following accents should be drawn progressively a little lower than that of the first accent to show that the first accent at the D_{i+1} level has the greatest relative pause in that level and that the others carry lesser divisions.

2.2 The Dichotomy Rule of Disjunctive Accents

In this example, the whole verse of Isaiah 5:1 is divided by *Silluq* and *Athnach* (D0 accents). The first half of the verse is the domain of *Athnach*, and its second half is the domain of *Silluq*. The second half domain of *Silluq* is divided by *Tiphcha* (D1 accent), and the domain of *Tiphcha* is again subdivided by *Tebir* (D2 accent). The domain of *Tebir* cannot be divided further because it consists of only one word.

The dichotomy process for the first half is a little different. The first half domain of *Athnach* is divided by both *Little Zaqeph* (remote disjunctive to *Athnach*) and *Tiphcha* (near disjunctive to *Athnach*). Since the domain of *Tiphcha* consists of two words, and since the first word in the domain carries a conjunctive accent, the domain governed by *Tiphcha* cannot be divided further. However, the domain of *Little Zaqeph* is further divided by *Pashta* (D2 accent). The domain of *Pashta* has two words, and the first word in the domain carries a conjunctive accent, so the domain governed by *Little Zaqeph* cannot be divided further.

Let us consider another example, 1 Samuel 14:42a:

(1) Determine all the disjunctive accents in a given verse.
    There are five disjunctive accents in 1 Samuel 14:42a: *Athnach*, *Tiphcha*, two *Great Zaqeph*s, and *Little Zaqeph*.
(2) Group the disjunctive accents according to their hierarchical level from D0 to D3.
    D0: *Athnach*
    D1: *Tiphcha, Great Zaqeph, Great Zaqeph, Little Zaqeph*
(3) Draw a dividing line for each domain.

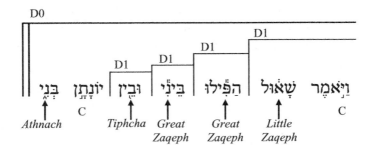

18   *Major Rules of Hebrew Accents*

1 Samuel 14:42a has four D1 accents, which is relatively rare. The domain of *Athnach* is divided by *Tiphcha* (near disjunctive to *Athnach*), two *Great Zaqeph*s, and *Little Zaqeph*. Because the domain of the two *Great Zaqeph*s consists of one word, *Great Zaqeph* replaces *Little Zaqeph* (see Table 4). The domain of *Little Zaqeph* consists of two words, and the first word in the domain carries a conjunctive accent, so the domain governed by *Little Zaqeph* cannot be divided further.

2.2.2 *Final Disjunctives*

Now let us turn our attention to the melodic features of accents. According to the hierarchy of disjunctives, under the domain of a Di level accent, several D$_{i+1}$ level accents may appear at times in a series without interruption by disjunctives of different levels. (However, conjunctives may come between these disjunctives.) In this situation, the first D$_{i+1}$ level accent presents the greatest relative pause, and the following D$_{i+1}$ level accents indicate progressively lesser pauses. This case presents a unique situation in that the last D$_{i+1}$ level accent appears just before the next level domain (i.e., the Di level) even though it itself carries the weakest pause.

In this situation, the last accent is called the "final disjunctive." It can be denoted as D1f if it is an accent of level one, as D2f if of level two, and as D3f if of level three (see Table 6). Regarding the concept of final disjunctives, Cohen comments: "the melody of the final disjunctive acts as a preparatory melody to the greater phrase terminator it precedes."[7]

---

[7] Cohen, *The System of Accentuation in the Hebrew Bible*, 40. See also Wickes, *Accentuation of the Twenty-One*, 31.

2.2 The Dichotomy Rule of Disjunctive Accents

Table 6 *List of final disjunctives*

Level	Final disjunctives
D1f	*Tiphcha* under the domain of *Silluq* and *Athnach*
D2f	*Tebir* under the domain of *Tiphcha*
	Pashta under the domain of *Little Zaqeph*
	Zarqa under the domain of *Segolta*
D3f	*Geresh* under the domain of all D2 accents

These designations are identical with Price's concept of "near disjunctive" (see Table 3).[8] Incorporating Price's terminology, we can schematically illustrate final disjunctives in light of the concept of "near and remote disjunctives," as follows:

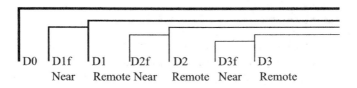

To illustrate, consider the following two examples:

Genesis 2:2a

---

[8] Price, *The Syntax of Masoretic Accents in the Hebrew Bible*, 29–30.

Genesis 11:9a

The function of the final disjunctives in both instances is quite close to that of conjunctives, in that both function as connectors between two different levels of disjunctive accents. However, their function is not identical to that of conjunctives in that they do not loosen the verse tension; they simply create a delay for a greater finale. Given their peculiar function, the final disjunctives may take the place of a conjunctive or another disjunctive of the same grade.[9]

2.3 Summary

In this chapter we investigated the hierarchy and dichotomy rules that govern the function of the disjunctive accents and the features of the final disjunctives. We also learned how to diagram the accentuation of a Hebrew verse by using these rules. The three steps presented for diagramming were: (1) determine all the disjunctive accents in a given verse, (2) group the disjunctive accents according to their hierarchical level from D0 to D3, and (3) draw a dividing line for each domain.

2.4 Exercises

Following the three steps outlined in Section 2.2.1, diagram the following verses and mark each level, including final disjunctives:

---

[9] Price, *The Syntax of Masoretic Accents in the Hebrew Bible*, 148–154.

2.4 Exercises 21

(1) Genesis 1:12

וַתּוֹצֵא הָאָרֶץ דֶּשֶׁא עֵשֶׂב מַזְרִיעַ זֶרַע לְמִינֵהוּ

וְעֵץ עֹשֶׂה־פְּרִי אֲשֶׁר זַרְעוֹ־בוֹ לְמִינֵהוּ

וַיַּרְא אֱלֹהִים כִּי־טוֹב:

(2) Isaiah 1:6

מִכַּף־רֶגֶל וְעַד־רֹאשׁ אֵין־בּוֹ מְתֹם

פֶּצַע וְחַבּוּרָה וּמַכָּה טְרִיָּה

לֹא־זֹרוּ וְלֹא חֻבָּשׁוּ וְלֹא רֻכְּכָה בַּשָּׁמֶן:

(3) 1 Kings 7:48

וַיַּעַשׂ שְׁלֹמֹה אֵת כָּל־הַכֵּלִים אֲשֶׁר בֵּית יְהוָה

אֵת מִזְבַּח הַזָּהָב וְאֶת־הַשֻּׁלְחָן

אֲשֶׁר עָלָיו לֶחֶם הַפָּנִים זָהָב:

(4) Judges 1:1

וַיְהִי אַחֲרֵי מוֹת מֹשֶׁה עֶבֶד יְהֹוָה

וַיֹּאמֶר יְהֹוָה אֶל־יְהוֹשֻׁעַ בִּן־נוּן

מְשָׁרֵת מֹשֶׁה לֵאמֹר׃

3 Substitutions of Disjunctive Accents (I)

In the previous chapters, we discussed the regular dichotomy patterns of disjunctive accents. In this and the following chapter, we will examine various dichotomy patterns with substitutions. These are not exceptional cases but were designed to present variegated musical neumes (i.e., a group of successive music pitches) in accordance with combinations of accents in the Tiberian tradition. This chapter will discuss substitutions of disjunctive accents at the D0 and D1 levels.

3.1 Disjunctives at the D0 Level

Under the domain of *Soph Pasuq*, the disjunctive accents at the D0 level are *Silluq* and *Athnach*. There is no final

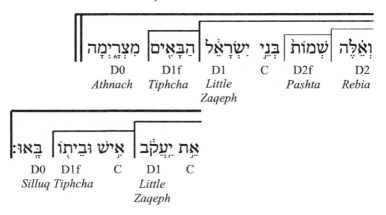

disjunctive accent in this level. Both *Silluq* and *Athnach* govern *Tiphcha* as the near subordinate segment and *Little Zaqeph* as the remote subordinate segment (see Table 3). This is illustrated by Exodus 1:1.

As this example indicates, the characteristics of the domains of *Silluq* and *Athnach* are similar, but not the same. In the Hebrew Bible, some short or verbless verses contain only the domain of *Silluq*. Furthermore, only *Athnach* permits the substitution of *Segolta* for *Little Zaqeph* in its domain (see Section 3.2.2). Consider the case of Genesis 10:14, which consists of three direct objects and a relative clause under the domain of *Silluq*.

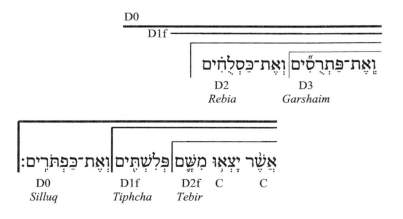

Similarly, Genesis 26:6 consists of only three words under the domain of *Silluq*.

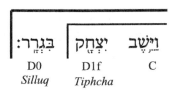

3.2 Disjunctives at the D1 Level

Under the domain of *Silluq* or *Athnach*, the disjunctive accent at the D1 level is *Little Zaqeph*, and the final disjunctive accent of this level (D1f) is *Tiphcha*. *Little Zaqeph* governs *Pashta* as the near subordinate segment and *Rebia* as the remote subordinate segment, while *Tiphcha* governs *Tebir* as the near segment and *Rebia* as the remote segment (see Table 3).

The domain of *Little Zaqeph* can be repeated. For example, in Genesis 2:5b, two domains of *Little Zaqeph* appear:

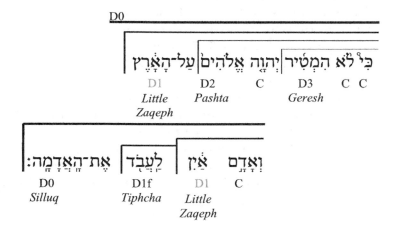

In Genesis 3:1b, there are three domains of *Little Zaqeph*:

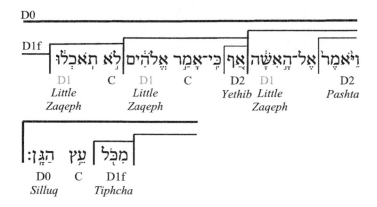

Having examined some relatively simple examples, let us now investigate more complicated cases that entail substitutions at the D1 level. These include substitution of *Great Zaqeph* for *Little Zaqeph*, *Segolta* for *Little Zaqeph*, and *Shalsheleth* for *Segolta*.

3.2.1 Substitution of *Great Zaqeph* for *Little Zaqeph*

Great Zaqeph substitutes for *Little Zaqeph* under two conditions: (1) when the domain consists of only one word or a one-word unit and (2) when the word in this domain is a short word. Here, the term "short word" refers to "a word containing only one syllable (without counting *shewa*) before the main stress."[1] Let us examine these two conditions in more detail.

The first condition for substituting *Great Zaqeph* for *Little Zaqeph* regards the word length of the domain. Thus, if a domain at the D1 level contains more than one word or word-unit, the substitution does not occur; *Little Zaqeph* always appears. For example, in Genesis 1:20a, two domains at the D1 level contain two words each, and *Little Zaqeph* rather than *Great Zaqeph* appears.

---

[1] Dresher, "The Word in Tiberian Hebrew," 95–111 (especially 105).

3.2 Disjunctives at the D1 Level

Let us now consider two additional cases from Genesis 3:10a and Numbers 31:30b that include a short word. On the one hand, in Genesis 3:10a, the domain of the D1 level includes only one short word. Thus, *Great Zaqeph* appears.

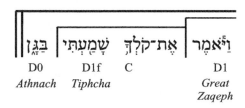

On the other hand, in Numbers 31:30b, the domain of *Great Zaqeph* contains only one word that is short. In this situation, the first domain of the D1 level takes *Little Zaqeph* because its domain consists of three words (וְנָתַתָּ֥ה אֹתָ֖ם לַלְוִיִּ֑ם).

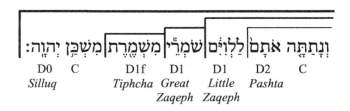

The second condition for substituting *Great Zaqeph* for *Little Zaqeph* regards the syllable length of the domain. If the word in the D1 domain is long, the word usually carries *Azla* or *Munach* (or *Metheg*) as a secondary accent. Consider the following examples from Numbers 28:20 and Deuteronomy 24:22:[2]

---

[2] Cohen, *The System of Accentuation in the Hebrew Bible*, 42–43.

Substitutions of Disjunctive Accents (I)

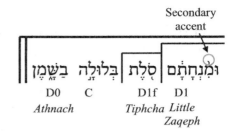

Here, the word in the domain of *Little Zaqeph*, וּמִנְחָתָ֔ם, is long because there are three syllables before the main accent. It carries *Azla* as a secondary accent.

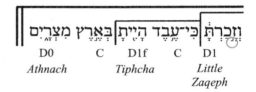

In this verse, the word in the domain of *Little Zaqeph*, וְזָכַרְתָּ֔, is long because there are two syllables before the main accent. It bears *Munach* as a secondary accent.

The situation in these two examples is similar in that the words in both passages are long words. The main difference between these two, however, is this: there is one closed syllable separated by at least one syllable from the main accent in Numbers 28:20, but not in Deuteronomy 24:22.[3] We will explore this in detail (see Section 5.3.2), but for now let us consider two more examples with secondary accents.

In Exodus 30:32, the word in the second domain of *Little Zaqeph*, וּבְמַתְכֻּנְתּ֔וֹ, has three syllables before the main accent and also includes one closed syllable (מַת) separated by one syllable (כֻּ) from the main accent. Thus, it takes *Azla* as a secondary accent.

---

[3] For the detailed discussion, see Breuer, פיסוק טעמים שבמקרא: תורת דקדוק הטעמים, 18–19.

3.2 Disjunctives at the D1 Level

In Deuteronomy 8:6, the word in the domain of *Little Zaqeph*, וְשָׁמַרְתָּ, has one closed syllable (מַר), but this syllable is adjacent to the main accent. Thus, it takes *Munach* as a secondary accent.

3.2.2 Substitution of *Segolta* for *Little Zaqeph*

Segolta can never substitute for *Little Zaqeph* in the domain of *Silluq*. However, this substitution can occur in the domain of *Athnach* under two conditions.

The first condition is that the domain at the D1 level consists of more than one word or a one-word unit. If this domain consists of only one word or a one-word unit, *Shalsheleth* appears in place of *Segolta* (see Section 3.2.3).

The second condition is a little more ambiguous. The domain of *Segolta* needs to be separated by at least one domain of D1 or D1f from the word stressed with *Athnach*.[4] This means that the longer the domain in which *Athnach* falls, the greater the probability that *Segolta* will appear.

Within this framework, it must be kept in mind that the occurrence of *Segolta* is not regular. Thus, it is possible that

---

[4] Cohen, *The System of Accentuation in the Hebrew Bible*, 44–45.

Segolta may not occur even when these two conditions are met. The domain of *Segolta* will not be repeated as the first domain of D1 level. Rather, *Segolta* governs *Zarqa* as the near segment and *Rebia* as the remote segment.

Let us now take a look at a few specific examples demonstrating the substitution of *Segolta* for *Little Zaqeph*. These examples show the practical application for the conditions for substitution and demonstrate that *Segolta* may not occur even when these two conditions are met.

In Genesis 1:28a, the domain of *Segolta* consists of three words (וַיְבָ֣רֶךְ אֹתָם֙ אֱלֹהִ֔ים), and there is the domain of *Tiphcha* (D1f domain) between those of *Segolta* and *Athnach*:

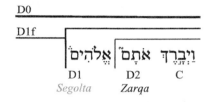

In Deuteronomy 19:5a, there are two *Little Zaqeph* domains and one *Tiphcha* domain between the *Segolta* and *Athnach* domains.

3.2 Disjunctives at the D1 Level

If we compare Genesis 36:39 with 1 Chronicles 1:50, we see that the appearance of *Segolta* is not mandatory, but that it may be introduced for the variation of musical neumes.[5]

---

[5] Cohen, *The System of Accentuation in the Hebrew Bible*, 45.

In Genesis 36:39:

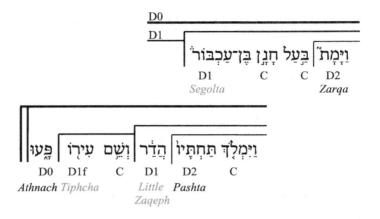

In 1 Chronicles 1:50:

3.2.3 Substitution of *Shalsheleth* for *Segolta*

As a rare accent, *Shalsheleth* appears seven times in the Hebrew Bible (Gen. 19:16, 24:12, 39:8; Lev. 8:23; Isa. 13:8; Amos 1:2; Ezra 5:15).[6] *Shalsheleth* is a substitute for *Segolta* when the domain of *Segolta* consists of only one word, which means that this accent always appears in the

---

[6] Wickes, *Accentuation of the Twenty-One*, 85; Price, *The Syntax of Masoretic Accents in the Hebrew Bible*, 84.

3.3 Summary

first word of a whole verse in the domain of *Athnach.* In the Twenty-One Books, this accent is always followed by *Paseq.*[7] Interestingly, three out of seven times, this accent appears on the verbal form of אמר within several different contexts: praying for God's miraculous intervention (Gen. 24:12), announcing God's dreadful judgment (Amos 1:2), and revealing God's unbelievable plan through King Cyrus' mouth (Ezra 5:15). The other passages express human emotion under imminent danger (Gen. 19:16, 39:8; Isa. 13:8). In each passage, *Shalsheleth* is intentionally introduced to draw special attention for Jewish homiletical interpretation.[8]

Leviticus 8:23a

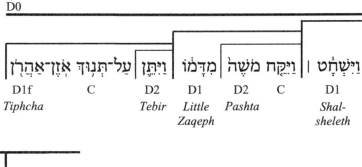

3.3 Summary

In this chapter, we examined various dichotomy patterns with substitutions at the D0 and D1 levels. These substitutions were designed to present variegated musical neumes. At the D1 level, we discussed three substitutions of disjunctive accents:

---

[7] Price, *The Syntax of Masoretic Accents in the Hebrew Bible*, 84.
[8] Weisberg, "The Rare Accents of the Twenty-One Books," (1966): 314–336; (1967): 57–70, 227–238.

substitution of *Great Zaqeph* for *Little Zaqeph*, *Segolta* for *Little Zaqeph*, and *Shalsheleth* for *Segolta*. These substitutions usually occur when a domain under the D1 level consists of only one word or a one-word unit.

3.4 Exercises

For each verse, mark the shape of the best disjunctive accents according to the hierarchy, dichotomy, and substitution rules of disjunctive accents, and then diagram the verse.

(1) Exodus 30:24

וְקִדָּה חֲמֵשׁ מֵאוֹת בְּשֶׁקֶל הַקֹּדֶשׁ
    D0   C   D1f   C   D1

וְשֶׁמֶן זַיִת הִין׃
D0 D1f   C

(2) Deuteronomy 9:28

פֶּן־יֹאמְרוּ הָאָרֶץ אֲשֶׁר הוֹצֵאתָנוּ מִשָּׁם
    D1   C   C   D2   D2

מִבְּלִי יְכֹלֶת יְהוָה
  D1   C   D2

לַהֲבִיאָם אֶל־הָאָרֶץ אֲשֶׁר־דִּבֶּר לָהֶם
    D0   C   D1f   D1

וּמִשִּׂנְאָתוֹ אוֹתָם
  D1   C

הוֹצִיאָם לַהֲמִתָם בַּמִּדְבָּר׃
  D0   C   D1f

4 Substitutions of Disjunctive Accents (II)

In the previous chapter, we examined various substitutions at the D0 and D1 levels. In this chapter we will continue to investigate substitutions of disjunctive accents and conditions under which these substitutions occur at the D2 and D3 levels.

4.1 Disjunctives at the D2 Level

The disjunctive accent at the D2 level is *Rebia*, and there are three final disjunctive accents of this level (D2f): *Pashta* (before *Little Zaqeph*), *Zarqa* (before *Segolta*), and *Tebir* (before *Tiphcha*). Each of these accents govern *Geresh* as the near subordinate segment and *Pazer* or *Great Telisha*, *Pazer*'s substitute, as the remote subordinate segment (see Table 3).

Let us consider a few examples of the three final disjunctive accents *Pashta*, *Zarqa*, and *Tebir* at the D2 level.

Genesis 1:2

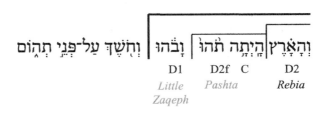

Genesis 3:17

Genesis 24:54

4.1.1 Substitution of *Yethib* for *Pashta*

In the domain of *Little Zaqeph*, *Yethib* can be substituted for *Pashta* under two conditions: (1) when the domain of *Yethib* consists of only one word or a one-word unit and (2) when the word in the domain of *Yethib* is stressed on its first syllable.

Consider the following examples from Exodus 12:4, 17; 32:20; 33:12; 34:3; and 34:18:[1]

Exodus 12:17

בְּעֶ֫צֶם הַיּ֥וֹם הַזֶּ֑ה

Exodus 34:18

כִּ֚י בְּחֹ֣דֶשׁ הָאָבִ֔יב

Exodus 32:20

וַיִּ֕זֶר עַל־פְּנֵ֥י הַמָּ֖יִם

Exodus 33:12

הַ֚עַל אֶת־הָעָ֣ם הַזֶּ֔ה

---

[1] The following examples are from Breuer, פיסוק טעמים שבמקרא: תורת דקדוק הטעמים, 19.

4.1 Disjunctives at the D2 Level

Exodus 34:3   Exodus 12:4

In Exodus 12:17, 32:20, and 34:3, the domain at the D2 level consists of only one word, but the word's stress is not upon its first syllable, so *Pashta* still appears. These passages can be contrasted with Exodus 34:18, 33:12, and 12:4, in which the main stress of the word is upon its first syllable and *Yethib* therefore occurs instead.

4.1.2 Substitution of *Pashta* for *Rebia*

In the domain of *Little Zaqeph, Pashta* can be substituted for *Rebia*, but there are no conditions for its substitution. Under the domains at the D1 level, the domain of *Rebia* can be repeated as Judges 2:20 demonstrates:

Judges 2:20

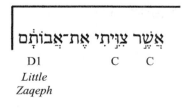

Regarding the repetition of the *Rebia* domain, Wickes suggests that three or more words are needed between two *Rebia* accents to provide "sufficient melody."[2] This suggestion makes sense because, as we already noted, substitution usually occurs at the place where the corresponding domain contains only one word or a one-word unit. Should the length of a melody not be enough, substitution occurs in order to provide a different melodic tone that makes that domain more distinctive than others. Under the domain of *Little Zaqeph*, *Pashta* substitutes for *Rebia* when the domain lacks sufficient melody, that is, when the domain of *Rebia* consists of less than three words.

Let us now consider some examples in which *Pashta* appears for *Rebia*, beginning with Judges 16:5a. There are three D2 domains together with one D2f domain in this passage. Furthermore, *Pashta* substitutes for *Rebia* in the third D2 domain because its domain consists of only one word (וּרְאִ֛י).

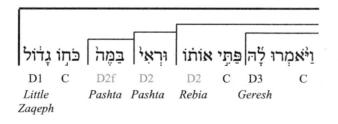

---

[2] Wickes, *Accentuation of the Twenty-One*, 78.

4.1 Disjunctives at the D2 Level

In Exodus 32:1, three D2 domains occur together with one D2f domain. *Pashta* substitutes for *Rebia* in the second D2 domain because its domain consists of two words, וַיֹּאמְר֣וּ and אֵלָ֔יו.

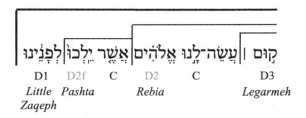

Sometimes *Pashta* occurs even when three or more words exist between two D2 accents. For example, in Genesis 27:37, there are three words between the first two D2 domains, but *Pashta* appears in place of *Rebia*. Strangely, although the domain of the second *Rebia* contains only a one-word unit by *Maqqeph*, its accent is not changed to *Pashta*.[3]

---

[3] Cohen, *The System of Accentuation in the Hebrew Bible*, 45.

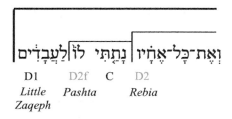

D1	D2f	C	D2
Little Zaqeph	Pashta		Rebia

Here, because *Legarmeh* appears in Exodus 32:1, it will be helpful to briefly discuss this accent. It looks like a combination of *Munach* and *Paseq* and usually appears as the subordinate segment (D3f) of *Rebia*, rarely of *Pashta* or *Geresh*. *Legarmeh* primarily occurs as D3f of *Rebia* under the following two conditions: 1) when the domain of *Legarmeh* contains only one word whose accent is placed on the first or second syllable, and 2) when at least two words exist to the left of *Legarmeh* under the domain of *Rebia*.[4]

For example, in Judges 8:12b, there is only one word (אֶת־שְׁנֵי) whose stress is placed on its second syllable in the domain of *Legarmeh*, and two words (מַלְכֵי מִדְיָן) remain to the left of the *Legarmeh* domain.

D2	C	D3f	D3
Rebia		Legarmeh	Garshaim

Nevertheless, these two conditions are not absolute, and many exceptions occur. For example, the conditions of Leviticus 7:20a and Judges 3:20a are identical in that there is only one word in the domain of D3f and two words to the left of the domain of D3f. In Leviticus 7:20a, *Geresh* appears as a D3f accent, but in Judges 3:20a, *Legarmeh* is found as a D3f accent.

---

[4] Breuer, תורת דקדוק הטעמים: פיסוק טעמים שבמקרא, 35–36.

4.1 Disjunctives at the D2 Level

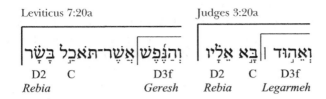

4.1.3 Rare Substitution of *Zarqa* or *Tebir* for *Rebia*

We have seen how *Pashta* can substitute for *Rebia* under the domain of *Little Zaqeph* due to the lack of sufficient melody. In these instances, *Pashta* appears as a transformation of *Rebia*. Similarly, if the domain of *Rebia* consists of less than three words, *Rebia* can be changed into *Zarqa* (when under the domain of *Segolta*) or into *Tebir* (when under the domain of *Tiphcha*). This phenomenon, which is sometimes called "musical assimilation," can be described in terms of the following transformations: *Rebia* > *Pashta* (under the domain of *Little Zaqeph*), *Rebia* > *Zarqa* (under the domain of *Segolta*), and *Rebia* > *Tebir* (under the domain of *Tiphcha*).[5]

In Exodus 12:29a, for example, the accent of the second D2 domain should be *Rebia*, but because there are fewer than three words between the first two D2 accents, *Rebia* is assimilated to *Zarqa*, making it identical with the following disjunctive accent.

וַיְהִ֣י ǀǀ בַּחֲצִ֣י הַלַּ֗יְלָה וַיהוָ֗ה הִכָּ֣ה כָל־בְּכוֹר֮ בְּאֶ֣רֶץ מִצְרַ֗יִם
D1   C   D2f   C   D2   D2   C   D3
Segolta   Zarqa   Zarqa   Rebia   Legarmeh

---

[5] Wickes, *Accentuation of the Twenty-One*, 88, 90–91; Cohen, *The System of Accentuation in the Hebrew Bible*, 52.

Consider another example, Numbers 14:40b. In this verse, because there are fewer than three words between the first two D2 accents, it is assimilated to *Tebir*, making it identical with the following disjunctive accent.

D1	C	D2f	D2	D2
Tiphcha		*Tebir*	*Tebir*	*Rebia*

4.2 Disjunctives at the D3 Level

The disjunctive accent at the D3 level is *Pazer*, and the final disjunctive accent of this level (D3f) is *Geresh*. Most verses showing the D3 level are long sentences. Furthermore, since the rules of the D3 level are "not as rigid and systematic,"[6] the disjunctive accents of this level can be easily transformed to other accents. In particular, *Geresh* can be replaced not only by other disjunctive accents like *Garshaim* or *Great Telisha*, but also by conjunctive accents.[7] Regarding this phenomenon, Price says that "before *Tebir* a *Geresh* is transformed to a *Darga* (or its substitute *Mereka*), before *Pashta* it is transformed to *Mahpak* (or its substitute *Mereka*), and before *Zarqa* it is transformed to *Munach* (or its substitute *Mereka*)."[8]

We will investigate *Geresh*'s special behavior in detail later with respect to two main phenomena: its transformation into another disjunctive (see Sections 4.2.1 and 4.2.2) and its transformation into another conjunctive (Chapter 5). For now, though, let us explore the typical use of *Pazer* and *Geresh* as accents.

---

[6] Cohen, *The System of Accentuation in the Hebrew Bible*, 53.
[7] Wickes, *Accentuation of the Twenty-One*, 117–118; Price, *The Syntax of Masoretic Accents in the Hebrew Bible*, 109.
[8] Price, *The Syntax of Masoretic Accents in the Hebrew Bible*, 110.

4.2 Disjunctives at the D3 Level

The basic forms of the D3 level are similar to the D2 level in two ways: 1) *Geresh* represents the near segment as D3f, and *Pazer* constitutes the remote segment as D3; 2) the domain of *Pazer* can be repeated just as that of *Rebia* is repeated in the D2 level. Let us consider two examples: Exodus 25:35a and 1 Samuel 25:39a

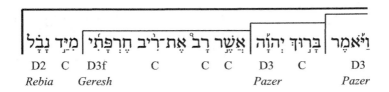

4.2.1 Substitution of *Garshaim* for *Geresh*

Having explored the typical usage of *Geresh* and *Pazer*, let us now examine some instances in which another accent substitutes for *Geresh*. *Geresh* is replaced by *Garshaim* when two conditions are met: (1) the word with *Geresh* is stressed on its ultima and (2) the word is not preceded by *Azla*.[9] The preservation of *Geresh* is illustrated by the following examples:

---

[9] Price, *The Syntax of Masoretic Accents in the Hebrew Bible*, 112. The following examples are from Breuer, פיסוק טעמים שבמקרא: תורת דקדוק הטעמים, 40–41.

Substitutions of Disjunctive Accents (II)

Genesis 1:12a (penultima with *Azla*)

וַתּוֹצֵא הָאָ֗רֶץ

D3f　C
Geresh　*Azla*

Exodus 14:27a (ultima, but with *Azla*)

וַיָּ֤שָׁב הַיָּ֗ם

D3f　C
Geresh　*Azla*

Genesis 14:9a (penultima with *Munach*)

אֵת כְּדָרְלָעֹ֗מֶר

D3f　C
Geresh

These passages can be contrasted with the following, which demonstrate the substitution of *Geresh* with *Garshaim*:

Exodus 5:7a (ultima with *Munach*)

לֹא תֹאסִפ֞וּן

D3f　C
Garshaim

Exodus 23:4a (ultima with *Munach*)

כִּי תִפְגַּ֞ע

D3f　C
Garshaim

4.2.2 Interchange of *Great Telisha* with *Geresh*

In other cases, *Geresh* can be substituted with *Great Telisha*. The interchange of *Great Telisha* with *Geresh* occurs under the domains of *Tebir, Pashta,* and *Zarqa* but not *Rebia*.[10] It is unclear under what conditions this substitution occurs, but the majority of these instances occur in the D3f domain when it consists of only one word. Consider the following:

Deuteronomy 26:12a

Genesis 13:1

Genesis 24:27

---

[10] Breuer, פיסוק טעמים שבמקרא: תורת דקדוק הטעמים, 33.

Sometimes, *Great Telisha* appears with a word stressed on its ultima, making it easily confused with cases in which *Garshaim* is substituted for *Geresh*. For example, in Leviticus 10:4, the word in the domain of D3 (קִרְב֛וּ) carries both *Great Telisha* and *Garshaim*.

As noted by Cohen, this confusion may reflect "a disagreement by the early authorities as to the proper disjunctive."[11] As a rare accent, *Great Telisha* may have been added late and therefore represent an alternative Jewish medieval tradition.[12]

4.2.3 Substitution of *Great Telisha* for *Pazer*

We turn now to substitutions for *Pazer*. Substitutions for this accent are much more common than the substitutions for *Geresh* described in the previous section. *Great Telisha* replaces *Pazer* when it would occur on the first or second word before *Geresh* or *Garshaim*, although this substitution does not occur when either of these words is long or joined by *Maqqeph*.[13]

For example, in 2 Kings 3:25, *Great Telisha* stands in the second word before *Geresh*. These two words (יַשְׁלִ֓יכוּ and טוֹבָ֜ה) are short and are not joined by *Maqqeph*.

---

[11] Cohen, *The System of Accentuation in the Hebrew Bible*, 55.
[12] Weisberg, "The Rare Accents of the Twenty-One Books," 57–70, 227–238.
[13] Price, *The Syntax of Masoretic Accents in the Hebrew Bible*, 113–114.

4.2 Disjunctives at the D3 Level

By contrast, in Exodus 12:27, *Pazer* appears in the second word before *Geresh*. The first word (זֶבַח־פֶּסַח) before *Geresh* is joined by *Maqqeph*, and the second word (וַאֲמַרְתֶּם) before *Geresh* is a long word.

4.2.4 Substitution of *Great Pazer* for *Pazer*

The substitution of *Pazer* with *Great Pazer* is rare and occurs only 16 times in the Hebrew Bible.[14] In part due to its

---

[14] Price, *The Syntax of Masoretic Accents in the Hebrew Bible*, 117. Num. 35:5; Josh. 19:51; 2 Sam. 4:2; 2 Kings 10:5; Jer. 13:13; 38:25; Ezek. 48:21; Esther 7:9; Ezra 6:9; Neh. 1:6; 5:13; 13:5, 15; 1 Chron. 28:1; 2 Chron. 24:5; 35:7. It

rarity, it is uncertain under which condition this substitution occurs. Wickes suggests that this transformation has the purpose of attracting special attention.[15] This is quite possible, especially because *Great Pazer*'s function is similar to that of *Shalsheleth*. Note the following two examples in which *Great Pazer* appears for *Pazer*.

Jeremiah 38:25

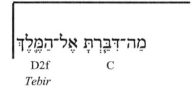

2 Chronicles 35:7

is interesting to observe that nine cases out of 16 are found in the postexilic literature. It occurs only once in the Pentateuch.

[15] Wickes, *Accentuation of the Twenty-One*, 114.

4.3 Summary

In this chapter we examined the substitutions of disjunctive accent at the D2 and D3 level.

Table 7 summarizes the substitutions discussed in the last two chapters (Chapters 3 and 4).

Table 7 *Summary of substitutions of disjunctives*

Level	Substitutions	Conditions
D1	*Little Zaqeph > Great Zaqeph*	(1) The domain consists of only one word or a one-word unit.
		(2) The word in that domain is short.
	Little Zaqeph > Segolta	(1) The domain contains more than one word.
		(2) That domain is separated by at least one D1 or D1f domain from the word stressed with *Athnach*.
	Segolta > Shalsheleth	The domain contains only one word.
D2	*Pashta > Yethib*	(1) The domain consists of only one word or a one-word unit.
		(2) The word in that domain is stressed on its first syllable.
	Rebia > Pashta	Under the domain of *Little Zaqeph*, the domain consists of less than three words.
	Rebia > Zarqa or Tebir	If the domain of *Rebia* consists of less than three words, this *Rebia* is changed into *Zarqa* under the domain of *Segolta*, or into *Tebir* under the domain of *Tiphcha*.
D3	*Geresh > Garshaim*	(1) The word with *Geresh* is stressed on its ultima;
		(2) That word is not preceded by *Azla*.
	Geresh > Great Telisha	Unclear, but the majority of this substitution occurs in D3f domain, which consists of only one word.
	Pazer > Great Telisha	*Pazer* occurs on the first or second word before *Geresh*; however, it does not occur when either of these words is long or joined by *Maqqeph*.
	Pazer > Great Pazer	Uncertain

4.4 Exercises

For each verse, mark the shape of the best disjunctive accents according to the hierarchy, dichotomy, and substitution rules of disjunctive accents, and then diagram the verse.

(1) Exodus 20:10 (cf. Exodus 20:10 *BHS*)

וְיוֹם הַשְּׁבִיעִ֗י שַׁבָּ֣ת לַיהֹוָ֣ה אֱלֹהֶ֑יךָ
      D0   C   D1f D1   D2

לֹֽא־תַעֲשֶׂ֣ה כָל־מְלָאכָ֣ה אַתָּ֣ה וּבִנְךָ֣ וּבִתֶּ֗ךָ
 D2   C   C   D3   C

עַבְדְּךָ֣ וַאֲמָתְךָ֣ וּבְהֶמְתֶּ֗ךָ וְגֵרְךָ֖ אֲשֶׁ֥ר בִּשְׁעָרֶֽיךָ׃
 D0   C   D1f   D1   D2f   C

(2) Genesis 21:14

וַיַּשְׁכֵּ֣ם אַבְרָהָ֣ם ׀ בַּבֹּ֗קֶר וַיִּֽקַּֽח־לֶ֣חֶם וְחֵ֤מַת מַ֙יִם
    D3   C   C   D3   C   C

וַיִּתֵּ֣ן אֶל־הָגָ֞ר שָׂ֧ם עַל־שִׁכְמָ֛הּ וְאֶת־הַיֶּ֖לֶד וַֽיְשַׁלְּחֶ֑הָ
   D0   D1f   D2f   C   D3f   C

וַתֵּ֣לֶךְ וַתֵּ֔תַע בְּמִדְבַּ֖ר בְּאֵ֥ר שָֽׁבַע׃
  D0   C   D1f   D1   C

4.4 Exercises

51

(3) Deuteronomy 22:6

כִּי יִקָּרֵא קַן־צִפּוֹר לְפָנֶיךָ בַּדֶּרֶךְ בְּכָל־עֵץ
D3f · · · · · · · · · · D3 · · · D3 · · · · · C · · · · · · C · · · C

אוֹ עַל־הָאָרֶץ אֶפְרֹחִים אוֹ בֵיצִים
D1 · · · C · · D2f · · · · · · D2 · · · · C

וְהָאֵם רֹבֶצֶת עַל־הָאֶפְרֹחִים אוֹ עַל־הַבֵּיצִים
D0 · · · · · · · D1f · · D1 · · · · · · · · D2f · · C

לֹא־תִקַּח הָאֵם עַל־הַבָּנִים:
D0 · · · · · · · D1f · · C

(4) 2 Kings 10:5

וַיִּשְׁלַח אֲשֶׁר־עַל־הַבַּיִת וַאֲשֶׁר עַל־הָעִיר
D3 · · · · · · · C · · · · · C · · · · · · · · C

וְהַזְּקֵנִים וְהָאֹמְנִים אֶל־יֵהוּא ׀ לֵאמֹר עֲבָדֶיךָ אֲנַחְנוּ
D1 · · C · · · D2 · · · · · · · · C · · · · · · C · · · · · · · C

וְכֹל אֲשֶׁר־תֹּאמַר אֵלֵינוּ נַעֲשֶׂה
D0 · · · · D1f · · · C · · · · · · · · D2f

לֹא־נַמְלִיךְ אִישׁ
D1 · · · C

הַטּוֹב בְּעֵינֶיךָ עֲשֵׂה:
D0 · · · · D1f · · · · · · C

52 *Substitutions of Disjunctive Accents (II)*

(5) Judges 2:12

וַיַּעַזְבוּ אֶת־יְהוָה | אֱלֹהֵי אֲבוֹתָם
D2   C   D3f   D3

הַמּוֹצִיא אוֹתָם מֵאֶרֶץ מִצְרָיִם
D1   C   D2f   C

וַיֵּלְכוּ אַחֲרֵי | אֱלֹהִים אֲחֵרִים
D2   C   D3f D3

מֵאֱלֹהֵי הָעַמִּים אֲשֶׁר סְבִיבוֹתֵיהֶם
D1   D2f   D2   C

וַיִּשְׁתַּחֲווּ לָהֶם
D0 D1f

וַיַּכְעִסוּ אֶת־יְהוָה:
D0   D1f

5 Conjunctive Accents

Until now, we have focused primarily on the disjunctive accents. In this chapter, we will explore the conjunctive accents and their connectivity preferences. Specifically, we will investigate the rules about which conjunctive accents are placed in a sequence before a disjunctive accent. Furthermore, we will examine secondary accents in detail: their definition, function, kinds, and replacements by conjunctive accents.

5.1 Preference of Conjunctive Accents

One of the main functions of disjunctive accents is to divide a phrase from the following phrase, that is, to serve as separators. By contrast, conjunctive accents function as a connector between disjunctive accents and do not exhibit any hierarchical order. This means certain conjunctives prefer to stand before certain disjunctives. Price outlines the preference of conjunctive accents as follows:[1]

As depicted in Table 8, most of the disjunctive accents take up to only three conjunctive accents. *Silluq* and *Tiphcha* permit at most one conjunctive to stand before it, and that conjunctive must be *Mereka*, whereas *Athnach*, *Little Zaqeph* or *Segolta* permits up to two conjunctives to precede it, and those

---

[1] Price, *The Syntax of Masoretic Accents in the Hebrew Bible*, 32–35.

54   *Conjunctive Accents*

Table 8 *Preference of conjunctives*

Disjunctives	Number of permitted conjunctives	Preference of conjunctives[a]
Silluq	0–1	*Mereka*
Athnach	0–2	*Munach*
Tiphcha	0–1	*Mereka*
Little Zaqeph	0–2	*Munach*
Great Zaqeph	None	–
Segolta	0–2	*Munach*
Shalsheleth	None	–
Rebia	0–3	*Munach* (first), *Darga* (second)
Pashta	0–2	*Mahpak/Mereka* (first), *Azla/Munach* (second)
Yethib	None	–
Tebir	0–2	*Darga/Mereka* (first), *Azla/Munach* (second)
Zarqa	0–2	*Munach/Mereka* (first), *Azla/Munach* (second)
Geresh	0–5	*Azla/Munach* (first), *Little Telisha* (second)
Garshaim	0–1	*Munach*
Little Pazer	0–6	*Munach*
Great Pazer	2–6	*Galgal* (first), *Munach* (second)
Great Telisha	0–5	*Munach*
Legarmeh	0–2	*Mereka* (first), *Azla* (second)

[a] The slash indicates another alternative. For example, before *Tebir*, either *Darga* or *Mereka* can come in the first place according to certain phonological conditions.

two conjunctives must be always *Munach*. *Rebia* takes up to three conjunctives: *Munach* in the first place, *Darga* in the second place, and *Munach* again in the third place. *Garshaim* takes nothing or at most one conjunctive, which is always *Munach*. *Legarmeh* takes up to two conjunctives: *Mereka* in the first place, and *Azla* in the second place.

5.2 Examples for the Preference of Conjunctive Accents · 55

Some of the disjunctive accents, however, can take more than three conjunctive accents. *Little Pazer* permits up to six conjunctives that are always only *Munach*, whereas *Great Telisha* takes up to five conjunctives, which are also always *Munach*. *Great Pazer* takes at least two to six conjunctives: *Galgal* must occur in the first place, and *Munach* appears from the second to the sixth places.

Furthermore, conjunctives can be categorized by position with respect to their governing disjunctive accent. A conjunctive in the first place is immediately followed by its governing disjunctive accent, a conjunctive in the second place is immediately located before another conjunctive in the first place, and so on. Notably, the only conjunctive that can appear from the third place to the sixth place is *Munach*.

Within this framework for categorizing the accents, Numbers 3:4 can be depicted as follows:

Disjunctive	first	second	third	fourth
יְהֹוָ֑ה	לִפְנֵ֣י	וַאֲבִיה֣וּא	נָדָ֣ב	יָ֣מׇת

Thus, the basic form for the appearance of conjunctives can be illustrated as follows:

> Sixth place Conjunctive + …+ third place Conjunctive + second place Conjunctive + first place Conjunctive + Disjunctive

5.2 Examples for the Preference of Conjunctive Accents

Having outlined the fundamental features of the conjunctives, let us now explore their characteristics in more detail by examining several case studies.

56   *Conjunctive Accents*

5.2.1 *Simple Examples*

We begin our exploration by looking at some simple examples of the information outlined in Table 8, in which the disjunctives prefer only one type of conjunctive.

Silluq

Genesis 1:1b   Genesis 1:3b

וְאֵת הָאָֽרֶץ׃   וּבֵין הַחֹֽשֶׁךְ׃

Tiphcha

Genesis 1:5b   Genesis 27:25b[a]

וַיְהִי־עֶרֶב וַיְהִי־בֹקֶר   וַיָּבֵא לוֹ יַיִן

[a] This combination (*Darga + Double Mereka + Tiphcha*) occurs only 14 times in the Hebrew Bible.[2]

Athnach

Genesis 1:1a   Genesis 40:16a

בָּרָא אֱלֹהִים   כִּי טוֹב פָּתָר

Little Zaqeph

Genesis 1:2b   Genesis 3:12b

וְרוּחַ אֱלֹהִים   אֲשֶׁר נָתַתָּה עִמָּדִי

---

[2] Wickes, *Accentuation of the Twenty-One*, 91. The 14 instances of this particular combination are Gen. 27:25; Exod. 5:15; Lev. 10:1; Num. 14:3; 32:42; 1 Kings 10:3; 20:29; Ezek. 14:4; Hab. 1:3; Zech. 3:2; Ezra 7:25; Neh. 3:38; 2 Chron. 9:2; 20:30.

5.2 Examples for the Preference of Conjunctive Accents

Segolta

Genesis 3:17a

לְקֹ֖ול אִשְׁתֶּ֒ךָ֒

Genesis 3:14a

כִּ֣י עָשִׂ֣יתָ זֹּאת֒

Rebia

Genesis 24:15a

וְהִנֵּ֤ה רִבְקָ֣ה יֹצֵ֔את

Numbers 4:14a

אֲשֶׁ֧ר יְשָׁרְת֣וּ עָלָ֥יו בָּהֶ֔ם

Garshaim

Genesis 1:11a

עֵ֣ץ פְּרִ֞י

Genesis 17:10a

זֹ֣את בְּרִיתִ֗י

Little Pazer

Jeremiah 35:15a (up to six *Munachs*)

וָאֶשְׁלַ֣ח אֲלֵיכֶ֣ם אֶֽת־כָּל־עֲבָדַ֣י הַנְּבִאִ֣ים ׀ הַשְׁכֵּ֣ים

וְשָׁלֹ֣חַ ׀ לֵאמֹר֒   Not *Legarmeh*

Great Telisha

Jeremiah 41:1a (up to five *Munachs*)

בָּ֣א יִשְׁמָעֵ֣אל בֶּן־נְתַנְיָ֣ה בֶן־אֱלִישָׁמָ֣ע מִזֶּ֣רַע הַמְּלוּכָ֗ה

Great Pazer

2 Kings 10:5

וַיִּשְׁלַח אֲשֶׁר־עַל־הַבַּיִת וַאֲשֶׁר עַל־הָעִיר

Ezra 6:9

Legarmeh

1 Kings 14:21b

וּשְׁבַע עֶשְׂרֵה שָׁנָה |

5.2.2 Complex Examples

Having looked at some simple examples of the conjunctive accents, now let us examine some more complex cases in which the type of conjunctive depends on placement.

5.2.2.1 Before Pashta

Pashta takes *Mahpak* or *Mereka* in first place and either *Azla* or *Munach* in second place. The situations in which these accents may be found before *Pashta* are as follows: for first place, *Mahpak* appears when there is any syllable including a *shewa* or *hateph* between two accents; otherwise, *Mereka* occurs; for second place, *Munach* is found when the accent falls on the first letter of the word; otherwise, *Azla* occurs.[3]

---

[3] Yeivin, *Introduction to the Tiberian Masorah*, 196–197; Wickes, *Accentuation of the Twenty-One*, 107.

5.2 Examples for the Preference of Conjunctive Accents

Examples of *Mahpak* appearing in first place occur in Genesis 18:31a, Exodus 18:15b, 21:13b, and 1 Chronicles 9:44a. In the last of these passages, there is a *Paseq* between two accents, but *Mereka* appears. Thus, *Paseq* is not considered as a syllable in this case.

Genesis 18:31a

הִנֵּה־נָ֣א ה֤וֹאַלְתִּי֙

Exodus 18:5b

אֲשֶׁ֣ר הִכֵּ֥יתָ בּ֖וֹ

Exodus 21:13b

וְשַׂמְתִּ֥י לְךָ֖

1 Chronicles 9:44a

עַזְרִיקָם ׀ בֹּ֣כְרוּ

Mereka stands in the first place in the following passages. In each instance, no syllable occurs between *Pashta* and *Mereka*.

Genesis 1:2a

הָיְתָ֥ה תֹ֙הוּ֙

Isaiah 1:3a

יָדַ֥ע שׁוֹר֙

Exodus 14:7a

שֵׁשׁ־מֵא֥וֹת רֶ֙כֶב֙

Exodus 14:27a

לִפְנ֣וֹת בֹּ֔קֶר

The accent *Azla* stands in the second place in these two passages:

Genesis 8:1b

וַיַּעֲבֵ֤ר אֱלֹהִים֙ ר֔וּחַ

Isaiah 30:10a

אֲשֶׁ֤ר אָמְרוּ֙ לָרֹאִים֒

Finally, *Munach* stands in the second place in the following two examples:

Genesis 13:14a

שָׂ֣א נָ֣א עֵינֶ֗יךָ

Exodus 12:42a

לֵ֣יל שִׁמֻּרִים֙ הוּא֙

60   *Conjunctive Accents*

5.2.2.2 *Before Tebir*

Tebir takes *Darga* or *Mereka* in first place and *Azla* or *Munach* in second place. The conditions in which a conjunctive may appear before *Tebir* are a little different from those of *Pashta*. For first place, *Darga* stands when there are two or more syllables including a *shewa*, *hateph*, or *Paseq* between two accents; otherwise, *Mereka* appears. For second place, *Munach* stands when the accent falls on the first letter of the word; otherwise, *Azla* occurs.[4]

Darga is found in first place in the following examples. Unlike the cases before *Pashta*, *Darga* is found if there is a *Paseq* between two words (see 2 Chronicles 20:8b).

Exodus 21:8a   Song of Songs 7:2a

בְּעֵינֵי אֲדֹנֶיהָ   מַה־יָּפוּ פְעָמַיִךְ

Genesis 1:22a   Isaiah 5:12a

וַיְבָרֶךְ אֹתָם   תֹּף וְחָלִיל

Mereka stands in first place, as illustrated by these passages:

Genesis 4:8a   Genesis 13:4a

וַיֹּאמֶר קַיִן   וַיִּקְרָא שָׁם

2 Samuel 19:34b   Micah 1:6a

וְכִלְכַּלְתִּי אֹתְךָ   וְשַׂמְתִּי שֹׁמְרוֹן

Notably, just before *Tebir*, a word-initial *shewa* has phonetic value (i.e., vocal *shewa*; see Exodus 21:8; Isaiah 5:12; Song of Songs 7:2), whereas a medial *shewa* after a long

---

[4] Wickes, *Accentuation of the Twenty-One*, 108; Yeivin, *Introduction to the Tiberian Masorah*, 201–202.

5.2 Examples for the Preference of Conjunctive Accents 61

vowel does not have any phonetic value (i.e., silent *shewa*; see 2 Samuel 19:34b; Micah 1:6a) when the number of syllables between the two accents is counted.[5] However, when *Paseq* stands between two words, *Darga* always occurs regardless of the existence of any syllable. For example,

Genesis 42:13a   2 Chronicles 20:8b

אֲחִים ׀ אֲנַחְנוּ   לְךָ ׀ בָּהּ

Azla appears in second place in these two passages:

Deuteronomy 26:2a   Numbers 13:3a

אֲשֶׁר תָּבִיא מֵאַרְצֶךָ   וַיִּשְׁלַח אֹתָם מֹשֶׁה

Finally, *Munach* stands in second place in the following examples:

Genesis 36:21a   Isaiah 1:5a

אֵלֶּה אַלּוּפֵי הַחֹרִי   עַל מֶה תֻכּוּ

5.2.2.3 Before Zarqa

Zarqa takes *Munach* or *Mereka* in first place and *Azla* or *Munach* in second place. A conjunctive may stand before *Zarqa* in several situations. In first place, *Munach* is most common whereas *Mereka* is rare. The rules governing the appearance of *Mereka* are uncertain, but *Mereka* usually occurs if *Metheg* and *Maqqeph* both appear in the final word stressed by *Zarqa* with no conjunctive in second place, if *Azla* precedes in second place, and if a *Metheg* in the final word or a *Paseq* follows. In second place, *Munach* stands

---

[5] For a detailed discussion, see Sung Jin Park, "The Validity of the Phonetic Value Changes of *Shewa.*"

62   *Conjunctive Accents*

when the accent falls on the first letter of the word; otherwise, *Azla* stands.[6]

On the one hand, the following examples show how
Munach appears in first place before *Zarqa*:

Exodus 8:17a (no *Metheg*)   Genesis 1:28a

כִּי אִם־אֵינְךָֽ   וַיְבָרֶךְ אֹתָם֮

Numbers 5:15a (no *Metheg*)   Exodus 20:9a (no *Maqqeph*)

וְהֵבִיא הָאִישׁ אֶת־אִשְׁתּוֹ֮   שֵׁשֶׁת יָמִים תַּעֲבֹד֮

On the other hand, the following sets of passages provide examples of *Mereka* occurring in first place:

(1) *Mereka + Zarqa*[7]

Exodus 6:6a   1 Chronicles 14:11a

אֱמֹר לִבְנֵי־יִשְׂרָאֵל֮   וַיַּעֲלוּ בְּבַעַל־פְּרָצִים֮

1 Kings 1:19a   1 Chronicles 21:12a[a]

שׁוֹר וּמְרִיא־וְצֹאן֮   נִסְפֶּה מִפְּנֵי־צָרֶיךָ֮

[a] Contra *BHS*, Yeivin thinks there is a *Metheg* in the word מִפְּנֵי־צָרֶיךָ.

---

[6] Wickes, *Accentuation of the Twenty-One*, 109–110; Yeivin, *Introduction to the Tiberian Masorah*, 205–207.

[7] There are only 10 verses in the Hebrew Bible with this combination of accents (Exod. 6:6; Exod. 30:12; Ruth 4:4; 2 Sam. 7:7; 1 Kings 1:19, 25; 1 Chron. 5:18; 14:11; 17:6; 21:12). Wickes, *Accentuation of the Twenty-One*, 100; Yeivin, *Introduction to the Tiberian Masorah*, 205.

5.2 Examples for the Preference of Conjunctive Accents 63

(2) *Azla* + *Mereka* + *Zarqa*[8]

Exodus 36:6a

וַיַּעֲבִ֥ירוּ ק֖וֹל בַּֽמַּחֲנֶה֮

Joshua 11:8a

וַיִּתְּנֵ֧ם יְהֹוָ֛ה בְּיַד־יִשְׂרָאֵל֮

Numbers 22:20a

וַיָּבֹ֨א אֱלֹהִ֤ים ׀ אֶל־בִּלְעָם֮

1 Chronicles 5:1a

וּבְנֵ֨י רְאוּבֵ֧ן בְּכֽוֹר־יִשְׂרָאֵל֮

It is worth noting that there are some exceptions to the use of conjunctives with *Zarqa* as described above. For example, in Joshua 18:14a, even though a *Metheg* does not occur in the final words stressed by *Zarqa*, *Mereka* appears in the first place and *Azla* occurs in the second place.

אֲשֶׁ֥ר עַל־פְּנֵ֨י בֵית־חֹרוֹן֮

Furthermore, the Hebrew Bible contains a few instances in which *Azla* and *Mereka* appear in the same word. One of these passages is Nehemiah 12:44:

לָא֨וֹצָר֥וֹת לַתְּרוּמוֹת֮

5.2.2.4 Before Geresh

The accent *Geresh* takes *Azla* or *Munach* in first place, *Little Telisha* in second place, and *Munach* from third to fifth place. The situations in which a conjunctive can occur before *Geresh* are relatively straightforward. For first place, *Munach* appears if the first letter of the word is accented; otherwise, *Azla* stands. However, if there are more than two conjunctives, *Azla* stands in first place and *Little Telisha*

---

[8] The combination *Munach* + *Mereka* + *Zarqa* is not attested in the Hebrew Bible.

occurs in the second place because *Little Telisha* always comes before *Azla*.[9]

The following examples illustrate the use of one conjunctive before *Geresh*:

Genesis 43:7a

חָח וָנָ֗זֶם

Exodus 35:22b

לָ֗נוּ וּלְמוֹלַדְתֵּ֗נוּ

Exodus 24:3b

וְכִבֹּ֗ר לֶ֗חֶם

Exodus 29:23a

וַ֗עַן כָּל־הָעָ֗ם

The following two passages provide examples of two or more conjunctives before *Geresh*:

Exodus 7:19a

Jeremiah 11:4

Disjunctive	first	second	third	fourth
Geresh	Azla	Little Telisha	Munach	Munach

בְּיוֹם הוֹצִיאִי־אוֹתָם מֵאֶרֶץ־מִצְרַיִם מִכּוּר הַבַּרְזֶל

5.3 Secondary Accents

Conjunctive accents most often function to connect words. However, they can also serve to stress certain syllables. In the Hebrew Bible, primary stress usually occurs on the ultima (the last syllable) of a word or on its penultima (the second-to-last syllable). However, in addition to primary stress, some

---

[9] Wickes, *Accentuation of the Twenty-One*, 112–113; Yeivin, *Introduction to the Tiberian Masorah*, 209.

5.3 Secondary Accents 65

marks are used to stress syllables that are placed neither on the ultima nor on the penultima. These marks are called secondary accents. Their main purpose is to slow down the reading of the syllable either phonetically or musically.

The most common secondary accent is *Metheg*, also called *Ga^{ʿ}ya* in the early masoretic tradition. It is represented by a short vertical stroke that is usually marked to the left of a vowel under a word. *Metheg* usually appears on long words carrying at least two syllables, or on long words possessing one syllable and a vocal *shewa* or a *hateph* vowel before the main accents. It also occurs several times in a phonological word connected by *Maqqeph* or in a word. The following two passages illustrate the several occurrences of *Metheg*.

Genesis 2:6 (3 *Methegs*),   Leviticus 1:5 (2 *Methegs*),

אֶת־כָּל־פְּנֵי־הָאֲדָמָה   הַכֹּהֲנִים

5.3.1 Two Groups of *Metheg*

Yeivin categorizes *Metheg* into two groups: phonetic *Metheg* and musical *Metheg*.[10] The purpose of phonetic *Metheg* is to phonetically ensure the exact pronunciation of the following consonant. Among other things, phonetic *Metheg* makes the following *shewa* vocal. For example, in Job 3:21 the word הַמְחַכִּים should be pronounced /hamhakkîm/ without a *Metheg*, but with a phonetic *Metheg* its pronunciation becomes /haməhakkîm/. Thus, in this case *Metheg* makes the following *shewa* vocal.

Whereas all phonetic *Methegs* ensure exact pronunciation, there are three kinds of musical *Methegs*: major *Metheg* (also known as light *Metheg* according to the later Ashkenazi tradition), minor *Metheg* (also known as heavy *Metheg*), and *shewa Metheg*. Major *Metheg* is in principle used to mark secondary stress on a long vowel, or on a long

---

[10] Yeivin, *Introduction to the Tiberian Masorah*, 240–264.

vowel before a *shewa*, in an open syllable; while minor *Metheg* is used to mark secondary stress on a short vowel in a closed syllable. *Shewa Metheg* is simply a *Metheg* marked next to *shewa* or *hateph* at the beginning of a word.

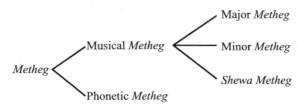

Here are some examples of major *Metheg*:

Genesis 22:12   Ezekiel 42:5

יָדְךָ֗   מֵהַתַּחְתֹּנ֗וֹת

Genesis 9:2 (before a *hateph* vowel),   Genesis 22:17 (with *Maqqeph*),

הָֽאֲדָמָ֗ה   כִּֽי־בָרֵ֗ךְ

Next, here are some examples of minor *Metheg*:

Deuteronomy 31:22   1 Samuel 30:5 (two *shewa*s)

וַֽיְלַמְּדָ֗הּ   הַֽכַּרְמְלִ֗י

Isaiah 57:8 (with a *hateph*   Leviticus 18:17 (with *Maqqeph*)
vowel)

וַֽתַּעֲלִי   אֶת־בַּת־בְּנָ֗הּ

Finally, consider some examples of *shewa Metheg*:

Deuteronomy 7:26   1 Kings 6:22 (with a *hateph* vowel)

תְּֽתַעֲבֶ֗נּוּ   אֲֽשֶׁר־לַדְּבִ֗יר

5.3 Secondary Accents

5.3.2 Replacement of *Metheg* by Conjunctive Accents

As indicated by the above examples, *Metheg* appears primarily in a word stressed by a disjunctive accent, but can occur by a conjunctive accent. However, when a word is stressed by a disjunctive, *Metheg* can sometimes be replaced by conjunctive accents, such as *Munach, Mereka, Mahpak, Azla,* and *Mayela.*

5.3.2.1 Replacement by Munach

Munach most often takes the place of *Metheg* in a word accented by *Little Zaqeph.* However, this replacement does not occur if the secondary accent is on the first letter of the word or in a condition to be a minor *Metheg* (that is, in a closed syllable).[11]

Genesis 3:1

אֶל־הָאִשָּׁה

Deuteronomy 9:26

וְנִחַלְתָּ֑ם

Leviticus 11:9 (on the first letter)

תֹּאכֵ֑לוּ

Exodus 32:13 (in a closed syllable)

אֶת־זַרְעֲכֶ֑ם

5.3.2.2 Replacement by Mereka

This conjunctive rarely takes the place of *Metheg* in a word stressed by *Tiphcha* or *Tebir.*[12]

Genesis 9:24

אֲשֶׁר־עָ֥שָׂה־לֹ֑ו

Jeremiah 8:18

מַבְלִיגִיתִ֑י

Deuteronomy 5:7

יִהְיֶ֥ה־לְךָ֖

Exodus 12:45 (with *Silluq*)

לֹא־יֹ֥אכַל־בֹּֽו

---

[11] Wickes, *Accentuation of the Twenty-One,* 80–82.
[12] Wickes, *Accentuation of the Twenty-One,* 91, 109.

5.3.2.3 Replacement by Mahpak

Mahpak takes the place of *Metheg* in a word (with שׁ) stressed by *Pashta*.[13] This case occurs only five times in *BHS*. (Song of Sol. 1:7, 12; 3:4; Eccles. 1:7; 7:10).

Song of Songs 1:7

שֶׁאָהֲבָה

Song of Songs 1:12

עַד־שֶׁהַמֶּלֶךְ

Ecclesiastes 1:7

שֶׁהַנְּחָלִים

Ecclesiastes 7:10

שֶׁהָיְמִים

5.3.2.4 Replacement by Azla

Azla replaces *Metheg* in a word stressed mainly by *Little Zaqeph* (for minor *Metheg*), at times by *Geresh* (for major *Metheg*). When *Azla* is used as a secondary accent as a minor *Metheg* with *Little Zaqeph*, it is also called *Methiga* ("an upper *Metheg*"[14]).

Genesis 18:18 (for minor *Metheg*)

וְאַבְרָהָם

Deuteronomy 29:28

הַנִּסְתָּרֹת

Leviticus 14:51 (for major *Metheg*)

וְאֶת־הָאֵזֹב

Exodus 16:15

וַיֹּאמְרוּ

Very rarely, *Azla* takes the place of *Metheg* in a word in first place governed by *Pashta, Zarqa,* or *Tebir.* For example, in Leviticus 25:46, under the domain of *Pashta, Mahpak* stands in the word in the first place, and *Azla* takes the place of *Metheg* in the same word as follows:[15]

---

[13] Wickes, *Accentuation of the Twenty-One*, 107.
[14] Wickes, *Accentuation of the Twenty-One*, 81–82.
[15] Yeivin, *Introduction to the Tiberian Masorah*, 197, 204, 207.

5.5 Exercises

69

וּבַאֲחֵיכֶם בְּנֵי־יִשְׂרָאֵל

Leviticus 10:12 (before *Zarqa*)   Isaiah 30:16 (before *Tebir*)

וְאֶל־אִיתָמָר ׀ בָּנָיו   וַתֹּאמְרוּ לֹא־כִי

5.3.2.5 Replacement by Mayela

Mayela substitutes for *Metheg* in a word stressed only by *Silluq* and *Athnach*. Since its shape is identical with *Tiphcha*, there are some debates about whether this secondary accent is really *Tiphcha*, or not.[16] But it is not surprising to observe this accent before *Silluq* and *Athnach* because *Tiphcha* hierarchically precedes these accents.

Jeremiah 2:31

אִם אֶרֶץ מַאְפֵּלְיָה

5.4 Summary

In this chapter, we focused on conjunctive accents and their preferences to connectivity with disjunctive accents. We did so because knowing the rules about the placement order of conjunctive accents before a disjunctive accent is crucial for understanding the masoretic accentuation system. We also examined important roles of secondary accents related to the main accent and possible replacements by various conjunctive accents.

5.5 Exercises

For each verse below, find the places where conjunctive and secondary accents might appear and mark their proper signs.

---

[16] Wickes, *Accentuation of the Twenty-One*, 73.

70   *Conjunctive Accents*

(1) Exodus 32:27

וַיֹּ֣אמֶר לָהֶ֗ם כֹּֽה־אָמַ֤ר יְהוָה֙ אֱלֹהֵ֣י יִשְׂרָאֵ֔ל

               C   C   C

שִׂ֥ימוּ אִישׁ־חַרְבּ֖וֹ עַל־יְרֵכ֑וֹ

             C

עִבְר֨וּ וָשׁ֜וּבוּ מִשַּׁ֤עַר לָשַׁ֙עַר֙ בַּֽמַּחֲנֶ֔ה

               C   C

וְהִרְג֧וּ אִישׁ־אֶת־אָחִ֛יו וְאִ֥ישׁ אֶת־רֵעֵ֖הוּ

               C   C

וְאִ֥ישׁ אֶת־קְרֹבֽוֹ׃

             C

(2) 2 Samuel 20:3

וַיָּבֹ֨א דָוִ֣ד אֶל־בֵּיתוֹ֮ יְרוּשָׁלִַם֒ וַיִּקַּ֣ח הַמֶּ֡לֶךְ

             C   C   C

אֵ֣ת עֶֽשֶׂר־נָשִׁ֣ים ׀ פִּֽלַגְשִׁ֗ים אֲשֶׁ֣ר הִנִּיחַ֮ לִשְׁמֹ֣ר הַבַּיִת֒

             C   C   C   C

וַֽיִּתְּנֵ֞ם בֵּית־מִשְׁמֶ֗רֶת וַֽיְכַלְכְּלֵ֔ם וַאֲלֵיהֶ֖ם לֹא־בָ֑א

               C

וַתִּהְיֶ֧ינָה צְרֻר֛וֹת עַד־י֥וֹם מֻתָ֖ן אַלְמְנ֥וּת חַיּֽוּת׃

             C   C   C

5.5 Exercises

(3) Esther 8:9

וַיִּקָּרְאוּ סֹפְרֵי־הַמֶּלֶךְ בָּעֵת־הַהִיא בַּחֹדֶשׁ הַשְּׁלִישִׁי

הוּא־חֹדֶשׁ סִיוָן בִּשְׁלוֹשָׁה וְעֶשְׂרִים

בּוֹ וַיִּכָּתֵב כְּכָל־אֲשֶׁר־צִוָּה מָרְדֳּכַי אֶל־הַיְּהוּדִים

וְאֶל הָאֲחַשְׁדַּרְפְּנִים־וְהַפַּחוֹת וְשָׂרֵי הַמְּדִינוֹת

אֲשֶׁר | מֵהֹדּוּ וְעַד־כּוּשׁ שֶׁבַע וְעֶשְׂרִים וּמֵאָה מְדִינָה

מְדִינָה וּמְדִינָה כִּכְתָבָהּ וְעַם וָעָם כִּלְשֹׁנוֹ

וְאֶל־הַיְּהוּדִים כִּכְתָבָם וְכִלְשׁוֹנָם׃

72   *Conjunctive Accents*

(4) 1 Samuel 1:11

וַתִּדֹּר נֶ֫דֶר וַתֹּאמַ֗ר

יְהוָ֨ה צְבָא֜וֹת אִס־רָאֹ֣ה תִרְאֶ֣ה ׀ בָּעֳנִ֣י אֲמָתֶ֗ךָ

וּזְכַרְתַּ֙נִי֙ וְלֹא־תִשְׁכַּ֣ח אֶת־אֲמָתֶ֔ךָ

וְנָתַתָּ֛ה לַאֲמָתְךָ֖ זֶ֣רַע אֲנָשִׁ֑ים

וּנְתַתִּ֤יו לַֽיהוָה֙ כָּל־יְמֵ֣י חַיָּ֔יו

וּמוֹרָ֖ה לֹא־יַעֲלֶ֥ה עַל־רֹאשֽׁוֹ׃

6 Minor Rules of Hebrew Accents

Thus far we have discussed the major rules related to disjunctive accents, their substitutions, and the key features of the conjunctive accents. In this chapter, we will examine several minor rules of Hebrew accents that are mainly related to deviations from the basic subdivision unit and stress crash (i.e., two consecutive stressed syllables). Specifically, we will look at the simplification and division rules, the spirantization (*sandhi*) rule, and the *nesiga* rule.

6.1 The Simplification and Division Rules

As noted in Chapter 2, a subdivision or phrase cannot be divided further when it contains only two words or only a single word or a one-word unit.[1] Here, the most basic subdivision unit is two words that consist of one conjunctive and one disjunctive accent. Since a disjunctive accent is considered stronger than any other conjunctive in terms of its stress strength and pausal value, this most basic subdivision exhibits an iambic structure (weak-strong) at the phrasal level. Isaiah 1:10, for example, illustrates a sequence of perfect iambic units at the phrasal level.

---

[1] Cohen, *The System of Accentuation in the Hebrew Bible*, 12.

73

However, there are numerous word units that deviate from this regular iambic pattern. So, we turn now to explore two important rules that account for deviation from the basic subdivision unit, namely the simplification and division rules.

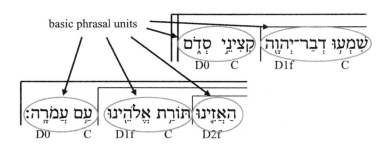

6.1.1 The Simplification Rule[2]

If a unit in the phrasal level consists of one disjunctive accent and two or more conjunctive accents (... C C D), the simplification process plays a major role for that unit.[3] Regarding this process, Cohen states: "Such a demanding system of multiple pauses of varying degrees of importance was not well-suited for oral presentation of the text.... Disjunctives were systematically replaced by conjunctives when it was felt that the former were too close to following disjunctives to permit a natural reading."[4]

The simplification process usually occurs under three conditions: (1) when the disjunctive accent is a final disjunctive that may be replaced by a conjunctive, (2) when the domain of that final disjunctive consists of two words,

---

[2] The examples in the section are from Breuer, טעמי המקרא בכ"א ספרים ובספרי אמ"ת, 49–53.

[3] Dresher, "The Prosodic Basis of the Tiberian Hebrew System of Accents," 36–37; Cohen, *The System of Accentuation in the Hebrew Bible*, 60–65; Breuer, טעמי המקרא בכ"א ספרים ובספרי אמ"ת, 83–107.

[4] Cohen, *The System of Accentuation in the Hebrew Bible*, 60.

6.1 The Simplification and Division Rules

and (3) when the final disjunctive immediately precedes its greater terminal disjunctive accents. The only exceptions to these conditions take place at the D0 and D3 levels. Simplification never occurs at the D0 level, while it widely occurs beyond the phrase length at the D3 level.

We turn now to examples of the simplification process. In the discussion below, the symbol CD represents a conjunctive simplified (or replaced) by a hypothetical disjunctive; the simplified domain is indicated by a dotted line.

6.1.1.1 The Simplification Process at the D1 Level

We begin our discussion of the simplification process by looking at several examples at the D1 level. In Genesis 28:20b, there are two consecutive conjunctive accents before *Little Zaqeph* (D1). Since the word אָנֹכִי with a conjunctive immediately precedes another word (הוֹלֵךְ) stressed with *Zaqeph*, the term אָנֹכִי satisfies the requirement to be stressed with a hypothetical final disjunctive. In this instance, the hypothetical final disjunctive would be *Pashta*, the final disjunctive of *Zaqeph*, and its preceding word (הַזֶּה) would carry *Rebia*, the remote segment of *Zaqeph*. We can schematically represent both the hypothetical, but possibly original, form of this verse alongside its simplified, actual form as follows:

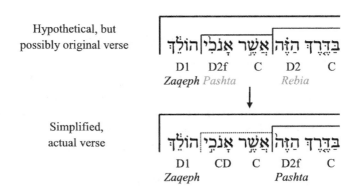

Genesis 26:28a provides another example of the simplification process at the D1 level. In this verse, there are two consecutive conjunctive accents before *Segolta* (D1). The accent on the word יְהוָ֖ה is not *Legarmeh*, but *Munach* followed by *Paseq* because *Munach* comes as a conjunctive of *Segolta* (see Chapter 5). Furthermore, the word יְהוָ֖ה immediately precedes another word stressed with *Segolta*, namely עִמָּ֑ךְ. So, יְהוָ֖ה would originally have carried *Zarqa*, the final disjunctive of *Segolta*, and the preceding word (רָאִינוּ) would originally have had *Rebia*, the remote segment of *Segolta*.

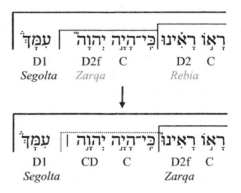

Finally, Leviticus 10:1b differs slightly from the two previous cases. There are two consecutive conjunctive accents under the domain of *Tiphcha* (D1f). Since the word לֹא immediately precedes another word stressed with *Tiphcha*, צִוָּה, this word would have originally carried *Tebir*, the legitimate final disjunctive of *Tiphcha*. But, its preceding word, זָרָה, can keep *Zaqeph* because *Zaqeph* is a D1 level disjunctive. Furthermore, the two words אֲשֶׁר and לֹא are short, so they may be connected

6.1 The Simplification and Division Rules

by *Maqqeph*. *Mereka* may also appear as a conjunctive of *Tebir*. Thus, the hypothetical representation of Leviticus 10:1b is as follows:

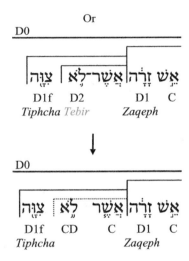

6.1.1.2 *The Simplification Process at the D2 Level*

We turn now to the simplification process at the D2 level. The simplification process at this level is not different from that at the D1 level. Under the domain of *Pashta, Zarqa*, and *Tebir* (D2f), the simplification process occurs if the final disjunctive of the D3 level immediately precedes the phrase-terminal disjunctive accent, D2f, regardless of the D3f phrase length. The same principle also applies to *Rebia*.

Let us look first at an example of the simplification process with *Pashta*. In Genesis 18:10a, which is under the domain of *Pashta*, the word אָשׁוּב immediately precedes the final word stressed with *Pashta*. Thus, אָשׁוּב can be treated as a D3f of *Pashta*. Since this word's stress is on its ultima, and since *Azla* is not a precedent conjunctive accent, *Garshaim* would have originally appeared in אָשׁוּב.

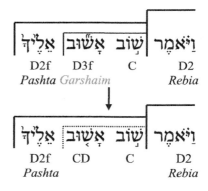

Exodus 17:6a shows the simplification process for the domain of *Zarqa*.

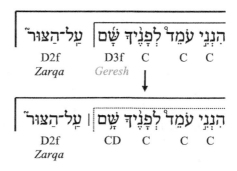

6.1 The Simplification and Division Rules

This simplification process for the domain of *Tebir* is illustrated by Numbers 35:18a. Because the word unit אֲשֶׁר־יָמוּת carries *Azla, Geresh* can be reconstructed for the word בּוֹ.

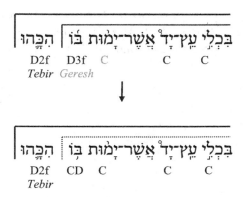

Lastly, the simplification process for the domain of *Rebia* remains the same. In Leviticus 23:27a, the word הַכִּפֻּרִים immediately precedes another word stressed with *Rebia*, הוּא. Because its stress is on its ultima, הַכִּפֻּרִים would have originally carried *Garshaim*, the final disjunctive of *Rebia*, and would have been preceded by *Munach*, not by *Azla*.

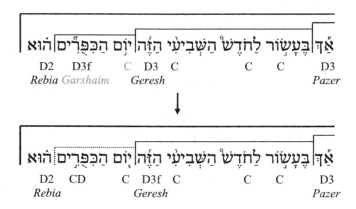

6.1.1.3 *The Simplification Process at the D3 Level*

The simplification process at the D3 level occurs without restriction by some of the conditions normally met at other levels and can occur beyond the phrasal length, too. For example, in Deuteronomy 2:32, which is under the domain of *Geresh, Pazer* is in the word סִיחֹן instead of *Great Telisha*, and *Munach* appears as a conjunctive of *Pazer* because the final word (לִקְרָאתֵנוּ) is a long word.

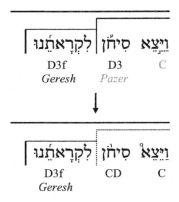

1 Kings 2:5 contains four consecutive conjunctive accents under the domain of *Great Telisha*. This disjunctive accent replaces *Pazer* (see Section 4.2.3) and is not repeated. Thus, two *Pazer*s would originally have appeared in the two words, שָׂרֵי and עָשָׂה.

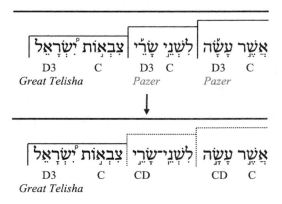

6.1 The Simplification and Division Rules 81

6.1.2 The Division Rule[5]

Having discussed rules for the simplification process, we turn now to the division rule. If a phrasal unit consists of two words with disjunctive accents, the division process plays a major role, especially in the domain of major disjunctives (D0 or D1).[6] This process is the opposite of simplification described in the previous section. A unit of two words with disjunctive accents results from a division process in which a disjunctive accent appears in place of a conjunctive accent. This process occurs especially when either of the words in the D0 or D1 domain is long, with "long" here referring to a word stressed after two vowels or a super heavy syllable with *Metheg*.[7]

Regarding the division rule, Cohen comments, "[This is] an attempt to [ensure] exact pronunciation of the text in situations where normal speech patterns would tend to increase carelessness of pronunciation .... Therefore, when such a case arose, it was often the practice to subdivide the simple phrase by introducing a disjunctive on the first word, thereby placing another major emphasis in the phrase and reinforcing the proper pronunciation."[8]

6.1.2.1 The Division Process at the D0 Level

We begin our discussion of the division process by examining cases at the D0 level. In Exodus 37:15a, the two words לָשֵׂאת and אֶת־הַשֻּׁלְחָן carry *Tiphcha* and *Silluq*, respectively, and the second word connected by *Maqqeph* is long. In this

---

[5] The examples in the section are from Breuer, טעמי המקרא בכ"א ספרים ובספרי אמ"ת, 89–94.

[6] Dresher, "Tiberian Hebrew System of Accents," 34–35; Cohen, *The System of Accentuation in the Hebrew Bible*, 80–83; Breuer, פיסוק טעמים שבמקרא: תורת דקדוק הטעמים, 89–94.

[7] Dresher, "Tiberian Hebrew System of Accents," 34; Park, *Typology in Biblical Hebrew Meter: A Generative Metrical Approach*, 72.

[8] Cohen, *The System of Accentuation in the Hebrew Bible*, 81.

case, *Tiphcha* replaces a conjunctive to reinforce exact pronunciation. The process can be illustrated as follows, with the divided domain indicated by a dotted line.

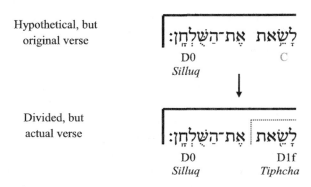

Leviticus 23:44 contains two consecutive disjunctive accents (*Tiphcha* + *Silluq; Tiphcha* + *Athnach*), and the words אֶת־מֹעֲדֵי and יִשְׂרָאֵל are long words. Thus, the division process takes place. *Mereka* appears as a conjunctive of *Silluq,* and *Munach* occurs as a conjunctive of *Athnach.*

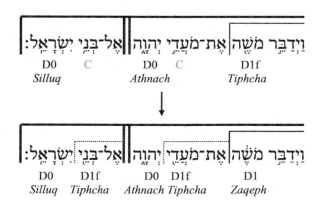

6.1 The Simplification and Division Rules

6.1.2.2 *The Division Process at the D1 Level*

The division process at the D1 level is identical to that of the D0 level. For example, Numbers 21:5 has two consecutive disjunctive accents, *Segolta* and *Zarqa*, and the two words carrying these accents are long. Thus, the division process occurs.

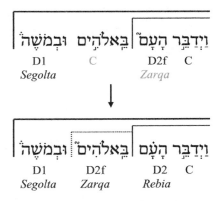

Deuteronomy 7:20 also shows the division process. In this passage, *Mereka* stands as a conjunctive of *Tiphcha*.

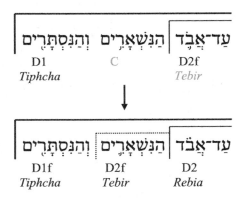

Finally, if we apply the basic phrasal unit rule along with the law of dichotomy and the division rule to Song of Songs 5:3, we can illustrate the division process as follows:

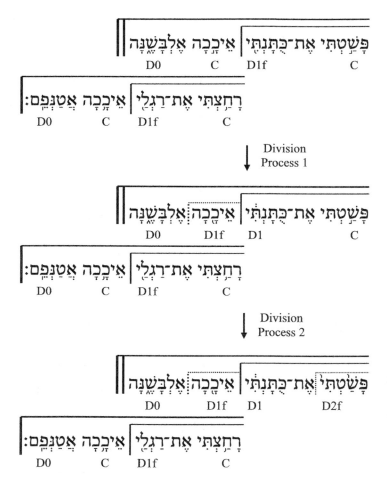

Two steps of the division process take place for this passage because the words אֶלְבָּשֶׁנָּה and אֶת־כֻּתָּנְתִּי are considered long in that both have two vowels before stresses. However, the word אֲטַנְּפֵם is considered short because it has only one syllable before the main stress (i.e., any initial *shewa*, including the *hateph* vowel, is not counted).

6.2 The Spirantization (*Sandhi*) Rule

While the simplification and division rules can account for many accentual patterns attested in the Hebrew Bible, they cannot account for all of them. Another important rule that helps to explain the Hebrew Bible's accentual patterns is the spirantization (*sandhi*) rule.

The main function of the disjunctive accents is to provide a pause between two words, whereas that of conjunctive accents is to connect two words. These functions are evident in the spirantization (*sandhi*) rule. When a word beginning with one of the six *begadkefat* letters (ב ג ד כ פ ת) is immediately preceded by a word ending with a vowel, spirantization occurs and the stops become softened fricatives. This is represented by omission of *Dagesh Lene* from the first letter of the word.

If a vowel-final word carries a disjunctive accent, spirantization does not occur because that disjunctive functions as a separator. However, if a vowel-final word carries a conjunctive accent, spirantization does occur. Both are illustrated, for example, by Judges 1:8:

	↑	↑
	Non-spirantization after *Pashta*	Spirantization after *Mahpak*

This process of spirantization confirms the function of conjunctives to phonologically connect two words beyond the word level.

6.3 The *Nesiga* Rule

Finally, we can account for some of the masoretic accentual patterns through the *nesiga* rule. Hebrew has two ways to avoid stress crash when two accents appear adjacently. One way is to retract the main stress on the first word, and a second is to cliticize (i.e., attach) the first word to the second word. Tiberian Hebrew accomplishes the latter with *Maqqeph* (see Appendix D.2). The former is explained by the *nesiga* rule in Hebrew and is identical with the "rhythm rule" in phonology. The phonological phenomenon of retracting stress to avoid stress crash is frequently attested in many of the world's languages.[9] Consider the following examples from English; in these examples, *s* represents a syllable with stress, and *w* represents a syllable with relatively weak stress.

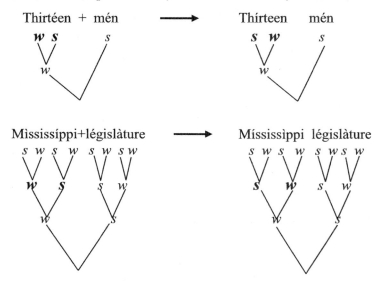

In the first example, the original stress on the second syllable of "thirteen" moves to the first syllable to avoid stress crash. Similarly, in the second example, the stress on the second-to-last syllable of "Mississippi" retracts to the first syllable to avoid having two consecutive stressed syllables.

---

[9] Hayes, *A Metrical Theory of Stress Rules*, 155–161, and "A Grid-Based Theory of English Meter," 367; Kiparsky, "Metrical Structure Assignment Is Cyclic," 421, 441; Prince, "Relating to the Grid," 31–46.

6.3 *The Nesiga* **Rule**

As already indicated, Hebrew also avoids stress crash by retracting word stress. Let us look at some examples of the *nesiga* rule from the Hebrew Bible.[10]

Leviticus 19:36

מָאזְנֵי צֶדֶק אַבְנֵי צֶדֶק ⟵ מָאזְנֵי צֶדֶק אַבְנֵי־צֶדֶק

Isaiah 34:12

יִהְיוּ אָפֶס: ⟵ יִהְיוּ אָפֶס:

Numbers 23:23

מַה־פָּעַל אֵל: ⟵ מַה־פָּעַל אֵל:

---

[10] Revell, *Nesiga (Retraction of Word Stress) in Tiberian Hebrew*, 39, and "*Nesiga* and the History of the Masorah," 37–48; Dresher, "Tiberian Hebrew System of Accents," 11, and "Stress Assignment in Tiberian Hebrew," 222; Hayes, *A Metrical Theory of Stress Rules*, 86–87.

Jeremiah 2:24 (exception)

As these examples illustrate, *nesiga* most often occurs in words with conjunctives, although *nesiga* sometimes occurs with a disjunctive accent as in Numbers 23:23. Furthermore, there are many instances in which the *nesiga* rule is not applied, as in Jeremiah 2:24; the rule often fails before monosyllabic words, particularly segolate nouns. No distinctive feature or reason for the failure of *nesiga* has yet been suggested in scholarly analysis of the Hebrew Bible.

6.4 Summary

In this chapter we discussed several minor rules of Hebrew accents: the simplification and division rules, the spirantization rule, and the *nesiga* rule. The simplification and division rules are based on deviation from the basic subdivision unit that consists of one conjunctive and one disjunctive accent. On the one hand, if a unit in the phrasal level consists of one disjunctive accent and two or more conjunctive accents, the simplification process plays a major role for that unit. On the other hand, if a phrasal unit consists of two words with disjunctive accents, the division process plays a major role, especially in the domain of major disjunctives (D0 or D1). The spirantization (*sandhi*) and the *nesiga*

6.5 Exercises   89

rules are mainly related to the functions of the disjunctive and
conjunctive accents and to stress crash, respectively.

6.5 Exercises

Reconstruct the original hypothetical verses according to the
simplification or division processes.

(1) Genesis 4:11

מִן־הָאֲדָמָה֙ אֲשֶׁר פָּצְתָה אֶת־פִּ֔יהָ

(2) Exodus 35:35

לַעֲשׂוֹת֙ כָּל־מְלֶאכֶת חָרָשׁ | וְחֹשֵׁב֙

(3) Numbers 8:11

וְהֵנִיף֩ אַהֲרֹ֨ן אֶת־הַלְוִיִּ֥ם תְּנוּפָה֙

(4) Numbers 30:13

וְאִם־הָפֵר֩ יָפֵ֨ר אֹתָם | אִישָׁה֙

(5) Leviticus 23:3

שַׁבָּת הִוא֙ לַיהֹוָ֔ה בְּכֹל מוֹשְׁבֹתֵיכֶ֑ם

For the following verses, identify all the disjunctive, conjunctive, and secondary accents, mark their signs, and diagram the
whole verse. SA represents a secondary accent.

90   *Minor Rules of Hebrew Accents*

(6) Exodus 16:20

וְלֹא־שָׁמְעוּ אֶל־מֹשֶׁה
D2   C

וַיּוֹתִרוּ אֲנָשִׁים מִמֶּנּוּ עַד־בֹּקֶר
D1   D2f   C   C

וַיָּרֻם תּוֹלָעִים וַיִּבְאַשׁ
D0   D1f   C

וַיִּקְצֹף עֲלֵהֶם מֹשֶׁה:
D0   D1f   C

(7) Deuteronomy 5:8

לֹא־תַעֲשֶׂה־לְךָ פֶסֶל ׀ כָּל־תְּמוּנָה
D1   C C   SA   SA

אֲשֶׁר בַּשָּׁמַיִם ׀ מִמַּעַל וַאֲשֶׁר בָּאָרֶץ מִתָּחַת
D0   D1f   C   D1   D2f   C

וַאֲשֶׁר בַּמַּיִם מִתַּחַת לָאָרֶץ:
D0   C   D1f   C

6.5 Exercises

91

(8) Deuteronomy 26:2

וְלָקַחְתָּ מֵרֵאשִׁית כָּל־פְּרִי הָאֲדָמָה

D2　　　C　　　　D3f　　　D3

אֲשֶׁר תָּבִיא מֵאַרְצְךָ

　D2　SA　 C　　 C

אֲשֶׁר יְהוָה אֱלֹהֶיךָ נֹתֵן לָךְ וְשַׂמְתָּ בַטֶּנֶא

D0　 C　　　D1f　C　　D2f　　C　　 C

וְהָלַכְתָּ אֶל־הַמָּקוֹם

　　D1　　　　D2f SA

אֲשֶׁר יִבְחַר יְהוָה אֱלֹהֶיךָ

　D1　　C　　D2f　　C

לְשַׁכֵּן שְׁמוֹ שָׁם:

　　D0　D1f　　 C

For the following verses, reconstruct all the best possible disjunctive, conjunctive, and secondary accents. A dark gray line represents a break and double dark gray lines represent a major break.

(9) Genesis 1:14

וַיֹּאמֶר אֱלֹהִים |

יְהִי מְאֹרֹת בִּרְקִיעַ הַשָּׁמַיִם |

לְהַבְדִּיל |

בֵּין הַיֹּום וּבֵין הַלָּיְלָה ||

וְהָיוּ לְאֹתֹת וּלְמֹועֲדִים |

וּלְיָמִים וְשָׁנִים ||

7 *The Divisions by Hebrew Accents*

So far, we have discussed how to diagram the accentuation of a Hebrew verse and the various rules that explain the accentual divisions. In this chapter, we will shift our focus to the linguistic representation of the divisions marked by the disjunctive accents from the word level through the sentence level and present some related topics, specifically prosodic analysis of the accentual divisions and performance structure.

7.1 Linguistic Representation of the Accentual Divisions

Scholars have long debated what the divisions marked by the disjunctive accents represent linguistically. They have offered at least three primary suggestions, all of which have validity: (1) to mark stress, (2) to provide musical notations, and (3) to express syntax (see Appendix A for more detailed discussion). Let us briefly evaluate each of these proposals.

Although marking stress is clearly a function of the masoretic accents, this cannot be their primary purpose. This is because several accents (more than 22%) are not imposed on a stressed syllable in a word but are pre- or postpositive. Given the limitation of this view, most scholarship has instead focused on musical notation and syntax.

Regarding musical notation, the accents arguably serve as a guide for cantillation. But there is a natural connection between providing musical notation and marking prosodic

94   *The Divisions by Hebrew Accents*

structure.[1] Their function does not seem to be limited to music in that the accents serve more broadly as a guide to the proper phrasing (or grouping) of the text in recitation and cantillation.[2]

Regarding syntax, scholars often attribute the divisions of the disjunctive accents to Hebrew syntax.[3] Mark Aronoff, for example, proposes that the accentuation system of the standard Tiberian Masorah was based on a theory of syntactic analysis.[4] It is true that there are numerous places where the accentual divisions do correspond to Hebrew syntax. At the same time, it is also true that many examples exist in which their divisions do not correspond with Hebrew syntax.

How, then, can we solve the problem of the accents' linguistic function? To do so properly, we must analyze several examples from the word level through the sentence level to figure out what linguistic representation exists in each level. This will enable us to sort through the proper relationship between prosody, syntax, and the masoretic accents.

7.1.1 *The Word Level*

We begin our analysis at the word level. As we do so, we need to remember that in the accentual system, "word" refers to a phonological word, not a grammatical word. A phonological word in Hebrew consists of a stem (i.e., host) and clitics, which include affixes (including particles), and short words with *Maqqeph*. An accent is placed on the stem of a phonological word in Hebrew, and a

---

[1] Dresher, "Tiberian Hebrew System of Accents," 1–52.

[2] Dresher, "Tiberian Hebrew System of Accents," 6.

[3] Aronoff, "Orthography and Linguistic Theory," 28–72; Avinum, "Syntactic, Logical and Semantic Aspects of Masoretic Accentuation Signs," 157–192; Cohen and Weil, "The Original Realization of the Tiberian Masoretic Accents," 7–30.

[4] Aronoff, "Orthography and Linguistic Theory," 52.

7.1 Linguistic Representation of the Accentual Divisions 95

cliticized word has no main accent, although it may have a secondary accent instead.

Orthographically, affixes include various particles such as the definite article, the interrogative markers, the negatives לֹא and אַל, the relative -שֶׁ, the direct object marker, the conjunction, and monosyllabic prepositions. They can also include prefixes and suffixes attached to verbs to mark the conjugation (e.g., perfect or imperfect), as well as pronominal suffixes attached to nouns, prepositions, and verbs.

To illustrate the division of words by stem and clitics, let us consider Genesis 41:20. This passage consists of nine phonological words that hold accents. The dark gray text represents clitics (i.e., affixes), while the light gray text shows stems (i.e., hosts).

וַתֹּאכַלְנָה הַפָּרוֹת הָרַקּוֹת וְהָרָעוֹת

אֵת שֶׁבַע הַפָּרוֹת הָרִאשֹׁנוֹת הַבְּרִיאֹת׃

In this example, אֵת is the monosyllabic direct object marker, and it carries a conjunctive accent. As an independent word, it is not cliticized (i.e., attached) to the following word with *Maqqeph*.[5] Because Hebrew particles are usually monosyllabic and are followed by the objects of those particles, by their nature, particles tend to be cliticized with *Maqqeph* or have conjunctives, but sometimes have disjunctives when the words following the particles are long.

Maqqeph is used to connect up to four grammatical words that are rhythmically close to each other into a phonological word unit. As a result, the main stress of the

---

[5] There seems to be no fixed rule under what condition a short word is cliticized into the following word with *Maqqeph*. For further discussion of this issue, see Appendix D.2.

96   *The Divisions by Hebrew Accents*

preceding word is drawn away by the vowel reduction of its final closed syllable. The main stress of the phonological word is placed on the stressed syllable of a stem word. Thus, the main purpose of *Maqqeph* is to prevent the addition of accents. In this sense, *Maqqeph* has a prosodic function, that is, it groups certain words together. Furthermore, the vowel reduction caused by the addition of *Maqqeph* is also prosodic in that it helps readers pronounce the word correctly. Clitics therefore can serve as a tool to make a phonological word and can be considered a unit of the prosodic hierarchy.

Let us consider two more examples. The phrases presented below from Genesis 23:19 and 20:14 mean the same thing but are represented differently. In Genesis 23:19 the direct object marker with *Maqqeph* takes *Segol*, but in Genesis 20:14 it takes *Ṣere* without *Maqqeph*. Thus, in Genesis 23:19 the two grammatical words אֶת and שָׂרֵה become a single phonological word due to the addition of *Maqqeph*, and because the stress of the direct object marker drops, its pronunciation is also shortened.

Genesis 23:19,

אֶת־שָׂרֵה אִשְׁתּוֹ

Genesis 20:14,

אֵת שָׂרֵה אִשְׁתּוֹ

7.1.2 *The Phrase Level*

Before extending our analysis to the phrase level, we first need to discuss spirantization and gemination as they relate to the masoretic accentuation system.

On one hand, when a vowel-final word carries a conjunctive accent, and when the initial consonant of the following word is one of the six *begadkefat* letters (ב ג ד כ פ ת), the stop changes to a softened fricative (see Section 6.2). This process is called spirantization. In the example below from Exodus 5:15, the initial consonants of the second and third words (which are preceded by vowels) undergo spirantization and have conjunctives.

7.1 Linguistic Representation of the Accentual Divisions   97

Spirantization
after conjunctives

On the other hand, 2 Kings 18:21 exhibits gemination (i.e., doubling) of the first letter (in this case a liquid consonant) of the word following a vowel-final word with a conjunctive.[6] Such gemination, marked by *Dagesh euphonicum* or conjunctive *Dagesh* or *Deḥiq*, makes the pronunciation of *shewa* audible, especially on a liquid or sibilant consonant. In this particular case, בָטַחְתָּ לְךָ is read as / bāṭaḥtāl ləkā /.

Gemination Spirantization
after a conjuctive

Although spirantization and gemination may seem like opposite processes, they are prosodically identical at the phrase level with respect to the pronunciation of two consecutive words.

Having discussed the prosodic function of spirantization and gemination, let us consider how these two processes affect construct phrases, a type of noun phrase. In Hebrew grammar, a construct phrase consists mainly of two constituents: the head (*nomen regens*) and its genitive (*nomen rectum*), which follows its head. Although the words in the construct chain and those joined by *Maqqeph* are closely associated with each other, there are several differences between the two. First, the words joined by *Maqqeph* are orthographically considered to be one phonological word,

---

[6] Gesenius, Kautzsch, and Cowley, *Gesenius' Hebrew Grammar*, 71; Yeivin, *Introduction to the Tiberian Masorah*, 289.

but the words in the construct chain are considered two phonological words, each of which carries its own main stress. Second, whereas with *Maqqeph* the preceding word usually undergoes vowel reduction as a clitic; in the case of the construct chain only the head noun in the construct state can differ morphologically from its absolute form.

Based on the syntactic relationship between a head and its genitive, we expect a conjunctive accent to come between them as a connector. For example, in Exodus 37:10, *Munach* occurs on the head noun (עֲצֵי):

$$\text{עֲצֵי שִׁטִּים}$$

"wood of an acacia tree"

However, there are some exceptions to the placement of conjunctive accents on the head noun. For example, in Exodus 10:13b, *Pashta* stands on the head noun, even

$$\text{וְרוּחַ הַקָּדִים}$$

"the wind of east" or "east wind"

though the head noun is in the construct state.

In this particular example, it is clear that one cannot treat the disjunctive accent as a divider because that would break the construct chain of this phrase.

Let us consider another example from Isaiah 40:13a. Following the reading of Targum Jonathan, Cohen translates this passage as follows:[7]

$$\text{מִי־תִכֵּן אֶת־רוּחַ יְהֹוָה}$$

"Who fixed the wind? The LORD did."

---

[7] Cohen, "Masoretic Accents as a Biblical Commentary," 6–8.

7.1 Linguistic Representation of the Accentual Divisions

Contrary to the conventional translation ("Who has directed the spirit of the LORD?" [cf. NASB]), which considers אֶת־ר֣וּחַ יְהוָ֑ה to be in the construct state, Cohen takes *Tiphcha* as a divider and translates the passage accordingly. This example vividly demonstrates how drastically the translation and interpretation of a passage can change depending on the treatment of the Hebrew accents' divisions. If we treat the accent as a punctuational marker expressing syntactic relation, Cohen's translation may be right. But, if we treat the accent as a cantillation marker indicating prosodic structure, then these two words must have a construct relationship because *Tiphcha* does not function as a main delimiter of the clause.[8] This would demonstrate that the accentual divisions are not always governed by Hebrew syntax.

To better understand the examples from Exodus 10:13b and Isaiah 40:13a, we need to review the division process (see Section 6.1.2). Since there are two consecutive disjunctive accents in the two examples above and the words הַקָּדִים and אֶת־ר֣וּחַ are both long, the division process occurs as follows:

Exodus 10:13b

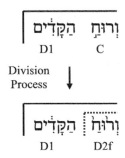

---

[8] de Hoop, "Stress and Syntax; Music and Meaning: The Purpose of Function of the Masoretic Accentuation System," 106.

Isaiah 40:13a[9]

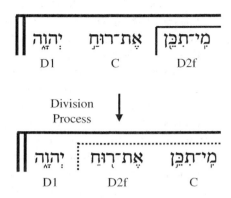

At first glance, these two construct chains seem to be exceptions to what we might expect. But it can be presumed that due to the division process, the original conjunctive accent of the preceding word would be replaced by a disjunctive accent to reinforce the proper pronunciation. From this we can conclude that, in most cases, the word preceding the construct chain carries a conjunctive accent for connectivity. Therefore, at least in the case of construct chains, the accents can express syntactic relation as well as prosodic representation.

7.1.3 *The Sentence Level*

Finally, having explored the accents' linguistic representation at the word and phrase level, let us consider some

---

[9] In Isaiah 40:13, since the furtive *patach* can be counted as a vowel (even if it is very short), the word אֶת־רוּחַ is considered as a long word. The furtive *patach* is an orthographic sign telling a reader not to ignore the guttural sound in pronunciation. See Gesenius, Kautzsch, and Cowley, *Gesenius' Hebrew Grammar*, §22f. There are four instances in the Pentateuch that show that the furtive *patach* is counted as a vowel in the accentual context of *Darga* and *Tebir*: רְבֻעַ הָיָה (Exod. 39:9); רֵיחַ נִיחֹחַ (Lev. 6:8); כָּל־הַנֹּגֵעַ בָּהֶם (Lev. 11:31); כִּי־פָתֹחַ תִּפְתַּח (Deut. 15:8).

7.1 Linguistic Representation of the Accentual Divisions   101

examples at the sentence level. On the one hand, Genesis 31:45 is a relatively short sentence whose placement of the *Athnach* perfectly matches the syntactic break between אֶבֶן and וַיְרִימֶהָ:

$$\text{וַיִּקַּח יַעֲקֹב אֶבֶן // וַיְרִימֶהָ מַצֵּבָה:}$$

Jacob took a stone // and set it up as a pillar.

On the other hand, in Deuteronomy 8:1 a major break occurs right before a relative clause:

$$\text{וּבָאתֶם וִירִשְׁתֶּם אֶת־הָאָרֶץ /}$$

$$\text{אֲשֶׁר־נִשְׁבַּע יְהוָה לַאֲבֹתֵיכֶם:}$$

You may enter and possess the land /
that the LORD swore to your forefathers.

In this example from Deuteronomy 8:1, the accentuation does not match the syntactical division that should occur after the second verb, וִירִשְׁתֶּם. In the Hebrew Bible a relative clause preceded by אֲשֶׁר is linked to by *Maqqeph* 252 times and by a conjunctive accent 469 times, but by a disjunctive accent 3,932 times.[10] The tendency for a relative clause to prefer a disjunctive accent exists because the length of the relative clause is usually long and mostly appears in the second half of a whole verse. From these observations we can conclude that the accents of Deuteronomy 8:1 do not correspond precisely to Hebrew syntax, but instead set apart a clause that explains the first half of the verse.

Another example in which the accents do not express syntax is found in Genesis 22:10. Here, the main division is designated by the major disjunctive accent *Athnach*, which is placed on the stressed syllable of אֶת־הַמַּאֲכֶלֶת. However,

---

[10] Price, *The Syntax of Masoretic Accents in the Hebrew Bible*, 316.

102   *The Divisions by Hebrew Accents*

according to Hebrew syntax, a major break should occur between אֶת־יָדוֹ and וַיִּקַּח. The second half of this verse as marked by the accents provides a reason for Abraham's behavior rather than marking a syntactical division.

$$ \text{וַיִּשְׁלַח אַבְרָהָם אֶת־יָדוֹ / וַיִּקַּח אֶת־הַמַּאֲכֶלֶת //} $$
$$ \text{לִשְׁחֹט אֶת־בְּנוֹ:} $$

Abraham stretched out his hand / and took the knife // to slay his son.

Genesis 18:7b demonstrates once again that the accents do not always have a syntactical function. In this passage, the syntactical break should occur after וַיִּקַּח. However, the accent-based division is placed after the second word בֶּן־בָּקָר, by means of the disjunctive accent *Geresh*.

$$ \text{וַיִּקַּח בֶּן־בָּקָר / רַךְ וָטוֹב} $$

He took a calf / fine and good.

The above examples demonstrate that the divisions marked by Hebrew accents are not syntactic. They can coincide with syntax, particularly in short and simple sentences, but do not always correspond to Hebrew syntax in longer and complex sentences. At the phrase level the divisions by accents correspond well to Hebrew syntax and prosodic representation, but at the sentence level the possibility of deviating from syntax increases as the length of the sentence increases. Put differently, the accentual divisions in shorter clauses and sentences are governed by syntactic and prosodic representations, whereas those in longer sentences are usually governed by prosodic representation.

The question is: Why does this tendency occur? To determine the reason for this tendency, we need to examine more closely prosodic representation.

7.2 Prosodic Representation of the Divisions[11]

As we examine prosodic representation, three important questions are in order: (1) What is prosodic analysis? (2) How does prosodic analysis differ from syntactic analysis? (3) How might prosodic analysis represent the divisions by Hebrew accents? In this section we address the issues raised by these questions and ultimately conclude that the Hebrew accents fundamentally mark prosodic divisions.

We begin by defining prosodic analysis, a topic of interest for linguistics, especially over the past few decades. According to prosodic theory, the mental representation of any spoken sentence can be divided into hierarchically arranged chunks, or grammatical constituents that are set apart by stress and intonation in speech perception.[12] Thus, the prosodic constituents (i.e., patterns of stress) of an utterance can be organized into a finite set of phonological units on the basis of morphological, syntactic, and semantic notions, but their arrangement is not necessarily identical to those of morphological or syntactical constituents.[13] Dresher thus states, "This adjusted syntactic structure is prosodic structure."[14]

A principal characteristic of prosody is its structural hierarchy. The hierarchy's lowest units (syllables or phonological words) are grouped into small phrases (phonological phrases), and then these small phrases are grouped again into larger phrases with tonal contours (intonational phrases), eventually composing an utterance. Let us now examine a few sentences that illustrate prosodic structure and distinguish it from syntactic structure.

---

[11] This section is adapted from my book, *Typology in Biblical Hebrew Meter*, 100–109.

[12] Nespor and Vogel, *Prosodic Phonology*, 1–3.

[13] Nespor and Vogel, *Prosodic Phonology*, 1–3.

[14] Dresher, "Tiberian Hebrew System of Accents," 8.

104   *The Divisions by Hebrew Accents*

This is the cat that chased the rat that ate the cheese.
$_S[_{NP}[$This $_{VP}[$is $_{NP}[$the cat $_S[$that $_{VP}[$chased $_{NP}[$the rat $_S[$that $_{VP}[$ate $_{NP}[$the cheese$]]]]]]]]]]]$
((This is the cat)$_I$ (that chased the rat)$_I$ (that ate the cheese)$_I$)$_U$.

The second sentence marks the syntactic break, whereas the third sentence presents its prosodic divisions based on the position of the intonational phrases (denoted by the subscript I) and the utterance (by the subscript U).

Consider also the following sentence:

On Tuesdays, he gives the Chinese dishes.

This sentence can be perceived in two different ways, depending on how one understands the syntactic function of "the Chinese," which could be taken as either a noun phrase or an adjective. Understood as a noun phrase, the sentence means "On Tuesdays, he gives dishes to the Chinese," but taken as an adjective, the sentence means "On Tuesdays, he gives the Chinese dishes" (i.e., Chinese pottery). In other words, the former means "He gives the dishes to the Chinese," while the latter means "He gives the Chinese dishes (to someone)."

How we perceive this sentence directly determines how we understand its structure. Consider the following diagrams of its possible syntactic and prosodic hierarchies (see Table 9). The following apparatus is used for the syntactic hierarchy: S: Sentence, PP: Prepositional phrase, P: Preposition, NP: Noun phrase, VP: Verbal phrase, V: Verb, Det: Determinative; for the prosodic hierarchy, U: Utterance, I: Intonational phrase, P: Phonological phrase, C: Clitics, and W: Word.

Although the words and their order are the same, the prosodic structures differ because the syntactic structures differ. Any given sentence, however, does not generate only one prosodic structure because it could potentially be grouped according to several different intonational phrases. Thus, Selkirk comments, "The relation between syntactic

7.2 Prosodic Representation of the Divisions 105

Table 9 *Comparison between syntactic and prosodic hierarchies*

Noun Phrase: "He gives the dishes to the Chinese"

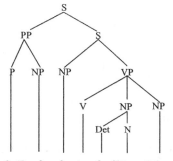
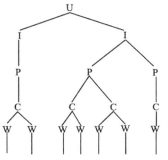

Adjective: "He gives the Chinese dishes (to someone)"

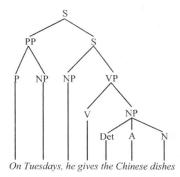
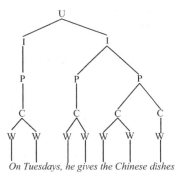

structure and all aspects of intonational structure can be depicted as a one-to-many mapping."[15]

Consider, for example, the sentence "Jane gave the book to Mary."[16] Its syntactic structure can be schematically denoted as follows:

---

[15] Selkirk, *Phonology and Syntax*, 285.
[16] Selkirk, *Phonology and Syntax*, 292–293.

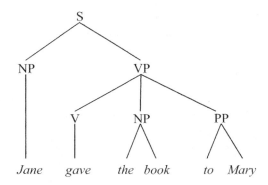

This same sentence's prosodic structure, however, can be represented by intonational phrases in several different ways, as follows:

[[Jane]$_I$ [gave the book to Mary]$_I$]$_U$
[[Jane gave the book]$_I$ [to Mary]$_I$]$_U$
[[Jane gave]$_I$ [the book]$_I$ [to Mary]$_I$]$_U$
[[Jane]$_I$ [gave the book]$_I$ [to Mary]$_I$]$_U$
[[Jane]$_I$ [gave]$_I$ [the book]$_I$ [to Mary]$_I$]$_U$

The above sentences consist of well-formed intonational phrases in which the constituents are syntactically connected to each other. However, there is no prosodic structure like [[Jane gave]$_I$ [the]$_I$ [book]$_I$ [to]$_I$ [Mary]$_I$]$_U$ since the words "the" and "to" as clitic constituents cannot be separated from the head elements "book" and "Mary."

It is worth observing that the syntactic structure and the prosodic structure of the final sentence are isomorphic (i.e., identical). We might also observe that the next two sentences are not well-formed prosodic structures.

[[Jane]$_I$ [gave]$_I$ [the book to Mary]$_I$]$_U$
[[Jane gave]$_I$ [the book to Mary]$_I$]$_U$

These two sentences do not represent well-formed prosodic structures because of the phrase compound "the book to Mary." In both examples, the noun phrase "the book" and

7.2 Prosodic Representation of the Divisions 107

the prepositional phrase "to Mary" do not bear any argument-head or modifier-head relation to each other.[17]

Let us compare some sentences from the Hebrew Bible that exhibit the same syntactic structure as the sentence "Jane gave the book to Mary," namely Genesis 14:12, 19:1, and 23:10.[18] The purpose of this comparison is to determine whether or not there is any correspondence between their syntactic and prosodic structures, for as the English examples above demonstrated, we cannot automatically assume a direct correlation between syntactic and prosodic structure.

Genesis 14:12

$$[\text{וְהוּא יֹשֵׁב}] \quad [\text{בִּסְדֹם:}]$$
D0   D1f   C

Genesis 19:1

$$[\text{וְלוֹט}] \quad [\text{יֹשֵׁב בְּשַׁעַר־סְדֹם}]$$
D0   C   D1f

Genesis 23:10

$$[\text{וְעֶפְרוֹן יֹשֵׁב}] \quad [\text{בְּתוֹךְ בְּנֵי־חֵת}]$$
D0   C   D1f   C

As the diagramming of these three sentences makes clear, their syntactic structures are identical (Subject-Verb-Adjectival phrase), but their prosodic structures are not.

---

[17] Selkirk, *Phonology and Syntax*, 293. In English, argument-head refers to a type of verb-noun (or noun-verb) compound, in which an argument of a verb is incorporated into the verb. For example, *breastfeeding, bartending,* etc. Modifier-head is a type of noun-noun compound, in which the final noun is modified by another noun. For example, in a construction such as *windmill,* the head element is *mill,* whereas the modifier element is *wind.*

[18] Dresher, "Tiberian Hebrew System of Accents," 21.

108   *The Divisions by Hebrew Accents*

Table 10 *Comparison between modern and Tiberian hierarchies*

Modern prosodic hierarchy		Tiberian accentual hierarchy	
Utterance	U	Bible verse	V
Intonational phrase	I	Main disjunctive phrase	Di, $0 \leq i \leq 2$
Phonological phrase	P	All disjunctive phrases	DP
Phonological word	W	Phonological word	W

Having demonstrated the difference between syntactic and prosodic structure for Hebrew, we must ask whether there is any correspondence between prosodic hierarchy and the Tiberian accentual hierarchy. Dresher was the first scholar to apply the levels of the modern prosodic hierarchy to the Tiberian accentual hierarchy[19] Building on and refining Dresher's work, I propose the following correspondence between the two hierarchies (see Table 10).

The correspondences I propose above differ from Dresher's in that I suggest a greater overlap between the two hierarchies than he does. Dresher thinks that intonational phrases (as defined in modern prosodic hierarchy) correspond to pausal phrases in Biblical Hebrew and thus suggests that pausal forms occur at the end of intonational phrases. However, because pausal forms appear not only at the end of the D0 domain, but also with lesser disjunctives and even with conjunctives, Dresher considers the overlap between intonational phrases and pausal phrases as only a "rough correspondence." This argument is problematic for at least two reasons.

First, Dresher connects intonational phrases with pausal phrases governed by disjunctives. However, because pausal phrases occur with lesser disjunctives, it is difficult to make a distinction between major and minor disjunctives. We must

---

[19] Dresher, "Tiberian Hebrew System of Accents," 8. For a similar argument, based on Selkirk's concept of the intonational phrase (*Phonology and Syntax*, 284–296), see Janis, "A Grammar of the Biblical Accents," 263–274.

7.2 Prosodic Representation of the Divisions

instead treat pausal form with minor disjunctives and conjunctives as exceptions that have the purpose of marking exegetically or rhetorically significant words or phrases, not to delimit intonational phrases.[20]

Second, contrary to what Dresher argues, some disjunctives cannot delimit texts as intonational phrases. For example, final disjunctives have no dividing force, and disjunctive accents on the initial word in a phrase or a sentence also have no dividing force because such accents also serve like a final disjunctive.

Given the limitations of Dresher's proposal, it is necessary to establish criteria for choosing major disjunctives whose function is to delimit the text as an intonational phrase. I propose three criteria for delimitation: (1) major disjunctive accents (*Silluq, Athnach, Little Zaqeph, Rebia,* and rarely *Segolta*) function as major delimiters, (2) final disjunctives have no dividing force, and (3) a disjunctive accent on the initial word in a phrase or a sentence has no dividing force because that accent also serves as a final disjunctive by preceding the next higher level of disjunctive.[21] Consider the case of Exodus 7:13:

וַיֶּחֱזַק֙ לֵ֣ב פַּרְעֹ֔ה וְלֹ֥א שָׁמַ֖ע אֲלֵהֶ֑ם // כַּאֲשֶׁ֖ר דִּבֶּ֥ר יְהוָֽה׃

Pharaoh's heart became hard /
and he did not listen to them, //
just as the LORD had said.

---

[20] Price, "Exegesis and Pausal Forms with Non-Pausal Accents in the Hebrew Bible," 1–21.
[21] de Hoop, "The Colometry of Hebrew Verse and the Masoretic Accents," 93–95.

In this verse, *Tiphcha* on the words שָׁמַע and כַּאֲשֶׁר serves as a final disjunctive; the phrases וְלֹא שָׁמַע and כַּאֲשֶׁר do not function as intonational phrases, while the preceding phrase וַיֶּחֱזַק לֵב פַּרְעֹה (governed by *Little Zaqeph*) can be treated as an intonational phrase. In addition, the initial word וַיֶּחֱזַק has *Pashta*, which precedes another disjunctive *Little Zaqeph*. Although a minor pause comes after the word וַיֶּחֱזַק, this pause cannot be a major division because it is under the domain of D2f.

Let us now look at a more difficult example, Numbers 1:18.

וְאֵת כָּל־הָעֵדָה הִקְהִילוּ /

בְּאֶחָד לַחֹדֶשׁ הַשֵּׁנִי /

וַיִּתְיַלְדוּ עַל־מִשְׁפְּחֹתָם לְבֵית אֲבֹתָם //

בְּמִסְפַּר שֵׁמוֹת /

מִבֶּן עֶשְׂרִים שָׁנָה וָמַעְלָה לְגֻלְגְּלֹתָם:

7.2 Prosodic Representation of the Divisions

> All the congregation they assembled /
> on the first day of the second month /
> and they were registered by the clans of their ancestral households, //
> according to the number of names, /
> from twenty years old and upward, by head.

In this verse, because the five words כָּל־הָעֵדָה, בְּאֶחָד, עַל־מִשְׁפְּחֹתָם, שָׁנָה, and וָמָעְלָה carry final disjunctives, the phrases including these five words do not function as intonational phrases, while the phrases including the words הַקְהִילוּ, הַשֵּׁנִי, אֲבֹתָם, שֵׁמוֹת, and לְגֻלְגְּלֹתָם can be treated as intonational phrases.

Finally, to demonstrate the validity of the criteria I have proposed, let us compare a passage's prosodic hierarchy with its accentual divisions. If the criteria proposed above are correct, we should see perfect correspondence between the two. This is exactly what we find. Thus, we can conclude that the divisions marked by the Tiberian accentuation system reflect prosody.

Table 11 *The prosodic hierarchy of Isaiah 1:10*

C: Conjunctive accent; D*i*: Disjunctive accent of *i* level; W: Word; V: Verse.

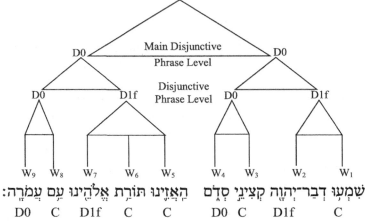

We will use Isaiah 1:10 as a case study. As will be seen in Table 11, it is expected that the prosodic analysis of Isaiah 1:10 and its accentual diagram should be isomorphic. Then, it is evident that the divisions by the Tiberian accentuation system are based on prosodic representation. Since Isaiah 1:10 is a poem, metrical balance based on parallelism is important.

Isaiah 1:10

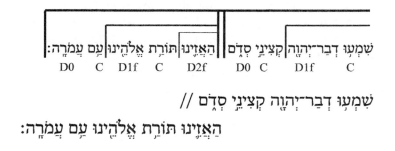

שִׁמְעוּ דְבַר־יְהוָה קְצִינֵי סְדֹם //
הַאֲזִינוּ תּוֹרַת אֱלֹהֵינוּ עַם עֲמֹרָה:

Hear the word of the LORD, rulers of Sodom, //
Listen to the Torah of our God, people of Gomorrah.

7.3 Performance Structure[22]

We have seen that the divisions by accents are governed by prosodic representation. Since prosodic structure includes syntactic structure, it is not surprising that some biblical verses correspond to syntactic structure as well as prosodic structure. Now we will discuss performance structure.

The purpose of a performance structure is to determine the prominence of boundaries in *real utterances* by obtaining empirical data such as pausal duration, transitional error

---

[22] This section is partially adapted from my book, *Typology in Biblical Hebrew Meter*, 85–87.

7.3 *Performance Structure* 113

probabilities, and parsing values.[23] Statistically, about 70% of all pauses occur at major constituent breaks.[24]

Recent scholarship has recognized that the division pattern in the Tiberian accentual system is quite close to performance structures as informed by the prosodic structure of sentences.[25] Its divisions are similar to performance structure in at least two respects. First, both are characterized by hierarchy. Second, and more importantly, the layouts in both cases are more or less symmetrical. This means that the most prominent break occurs at the midpoint of a sentence, whereas those next in prominence take place in the midpoint of the half sentence circumscribed by the most prominent break. Performance structures can be schematically depicted as follows (see Table 12):[26]

In these two examples, the number between the words indicates the pause duration percentage. In the first sentence, the number 25 between "cons" and "to" refers to 25% of the sentence's pausal breaks that take place when the whole sentence is spoken. In other words, the speaker stops at this point for one-quarter of the whole time spent during the reading of the sentence. This juncture is by far the longest break or the most prominent pause, and it is located

---

[23] Gee and Grosjean, "Performance Structures: A Psycholinguistic and Linguistic Appraisal," 411–458; Grosjean, Grosjean, and Lane, "The Patterns of Silence: Performance Structures in Sentence Production," 58–81; Keller, "Revisiting the Status of Speech Rhythm," 727–730.

[24] Grosjean and Deschamps, "Analyse contrastive des variables temporelles de l'anglais et du francais: Vitesse de parole et variables composantes, phénomènes d'hésitation," 144–184; Christophe, Nespor, Guasti and van Ooyen, "Prosodic Structure and Syntactic Acquisition: The Case of the Head-Direction Parameter," 211–220.

[25] Although the performance structures have been researched by psycholinguists, it was Janis and Dresher who first applied the pattern of the performance structures to the division pattern by Hebrew accents. Janis, "A Grammar of the Biblical Accents," 23–86; Dresher, "Tiberian Hebrew System of Accents," 1–52.

[26] Gee and Grosjean, "Performance Structures," 415.

Table 12 *Examples of performance structure*

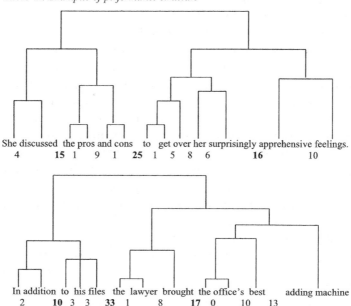

approximately in the middle of the sentence. The two second-longest breaks, marked by the numbers 15 and 16, take place approximately halfway between the most prominent pause and the boundaries of the sentence, resulting in a symmetrical structure. In the second sentence, the longest break is skewed toward the beginning, but the second-longest ones remain centered.

Of course, we cannot prove with certainty that the two divisions by Hebrew accents and the performance structure are identical because we do not know how ancient Hebrew speakers actually read their biblical texts. At the very least, however, we do know that the division patterns based on the rule of dichotomy for the Hebrew accents and the pause duration percentage in performance structures share the

7.4 Summary

same linguistic concept regarding the prosodic structures of a sentence (i.e., pause in real speech). Thus, the major purpose of the Tiberian system's accents seems to be to mark pause for proper recitation.[27]

7.4 Summary

In this chapter, we demonstrated that the divisions marked by the Tiberian accents correspond with prosodic divisions and suggested three criteria for delimitation: (1) major disjunctive accents (*Silluq, Athnach, Little Zaqeph, Rebia*, and rarely *Segolta*) function as major delimiters, (2) final disjunctives have no dividing force, and (3) a disjunctive accent on the initial word in a phrase or a sentence does not have dividing force. Notably, these accentual divisions correspond with performance structure in light of pausal duration in speech. This shows that the primary purpose of the accents is to mark the proper recitation of the text.

---

[27] This fact may explain the reason why parallelism was used as a dominant feature of Biblical Hebrew poetry, assuming that the masoretic accents represent very ancient tradition.

8 *The Exegetical Roles of the Divisions*

In the last chapter we determined that the divisions marked by the masoretic accents correspond with prosodic divisions and performance structure. This led us to conclude that the primary purpose of the accents is to mark the proper recitation of the text. In light of this, an important question remains: What role do the accents play in exegesis of the Hebrew Bible? This chapter investigates this question and concludes that the accents can help clarify ambiguous meanings, emphasize certain words or phrases, and create dramatic effect in biblical narrative.

8.1 Clarifying Ambiguous Meanings

The first exegetical role of the divisions by accents is to resolve ambiguity in a given verse. In some passages the Hebrew text could, at first glance, be read in more than one way. However, in many of these instances, careful attention to the accentuation of the passage reveals the correct reading of the text. The following examples from Numbers 25:9, Genesis 24:34, Isaiah 40:3a, and Isaiah 53:2 demonstrate the accents' usefulness in clarifying ambiguity.

Numbers 25:9 records the number of people who died because of plague. When read without the accents, this

8.1 Clarifying Ambiguous Meanings

passage can be understood in two ways: either 20,004 people or 24,000 people.[1]

$$\text{(אַרְבָּעָה) (וְעֶשְׂרִים אָלֶף)}$$

Literally "4 and 20-thousand," that is "20,004 people" (cf. the LXX)

$$\text{(אַרְבָּעָה וְעֶשְׂרִים) (אָלֶף)}$$

"24 thousand people"

However, according to the divisions by Hebrew accents, the first two words are closely connected by *Mereka*. Thus, the correct number would be 24,000 people.

$$\text{(אַרְבָּעָה וְעֶשְׂרִים) (אָלֶף)}$$

A second example comes from Genesis 24:34. When read without accents, the subject who speaks in this verse is ambiguous.

$$\text{וַיֹּאמַר עֶבֶד אַבְרָהָם אָנֹכִי:}$$

Grammatically, there are three viable options for the subject in this verse:

(1) "He" (He said, "I am a servant of Abraham.");
(2) "A servant" (A servant said, "I am Abraham.");
(3) "A servant of Abraham" (A servant of Abraham said, "It is I.").

According to the divisions by accents, however, the sentence's subject is clearly "he," and the complement of the direct

---

[1] Johnson, *Chanting the Hebrew Bible*, 22.

118   *The Exegetical Roles of the Divisions*

speech is emphatic. Thus, the correct translation would be "He said, 'A servant of Abraham, I am.'"[2]

$$\text{(וַיֹּאמֶר) (עֶבֶד אַבְרָהָם) (אָנֹכִי:)}$$

Yet another example is provided by Isaiah 40:3a, which can be translated in two different ways when read without any accentuation.

$$\text{(קוֹל קוֹרֵא בַּמִּדְבָּר) (פַּנּוּ דֶּרֶךְ יְהוָה)}$$

"A voice is calling in the wilderness, 'Clear the way for the LORD!'"

$$\text{(קוֹל קוֹרֵא) (בַּמִּדְבָּר פַּנּוּ דֶּרֶךְ יְהוָה)}$$

"A voice is calling, 'In the wilderness, clear the way for the LORD!'"

According to the divisions by accents, it is evident that the place to clear the way for the LORD is "the wilderness."[3]

$$\text{קוֹל קוֹרֵא /}$$
$$\text{בַּמִּדְבָּר פַּנּוּ דֶּרֶךְ יְהוָה //}$$
$$\text{יַשְּׁרוּ בָּעֲרָבָה /}$$
$$\text{מְסִלָּה לֵאלֹהֵינוּ:}$$

A voice is calling, /
"In the wilderness, clear the way for the LORD! //
Make straight in the desert /
a highway for our God!"

In this example, the accentual divisions display an excellent synonymous parallelism via several synonym pairs: בַּמִּדְבָּר and

---

[2] Johnson, *Chanting the Hebrew Bible*, 22.

[3] Johnson, Chanting the Hebrew Bible, 22.

8.1 Clarifying Ambiguous Meanings

119

בְּעֲרָבָה, דֶּרֶךְ and יְהוָה, מְסִלָּה and לֵאלֹהֵינוּ, פַּנּוּ and יְשְׁרוּ. However, in John 1:23 the Byzantine Textform and most English Bible translations quote Isaiah 40:3 by placing the phrase "in the wilderness" into the first phrase (He said, "I am a voice of one crying in the wilderness, 'Make straight the way of the LORD,' as Isaiah the prophet said;" ἔφη Ἐγὼ φωνὴ βοῶντος ἐν τῇ ἐρήμῳ·Εὐθύνατε τὴν ὁδὸν κυρίου, καθὼς εἶπεν Ἠσαΐας ὁ προφήτης.) and present John the Baptist's self-identification in the wilderness.

As a fourth and final example, according to Hebrew accents Isaiah 53:2 should be divided as follows:[4]

$$וַיַּעַל כַּיּוֹנֵק לְפָנָיו /$$

$$וְכַשֹּׁרֶשׁ מֵאֶרֶץ צִיָּה /$$

$$לֹא־תֹאַר לוֹ וְלֹא הָדָר //$$

$$וְנִרְאֵהוּ וְלֹא־מַרְאֶה וְנֶחְמְדֵהוּ׃$$

There is little debate over the translation of the first two lines, but the final two lines are unclear in their meaning. The NASB translates: "He has no stately form or majesty that we should look upon Him, Nor appearance that we should be attracted to Him," and the NIV similarly reads: "He had no beauty or majesty to attract us to him, nothing in his appearance that we should desire him." These two translations take הָדָר וְנִרְאֵהוּ as an adjective clause ("majesty that we should look upon him" [NASB]) or phrase ("majesty to attract us to him" [NIV]). According to these translations, the logical divisions by accent should be like this:

$$לֹא־תֹאַר לוֹ וְלֹא הָדָר וְנִרְאֵהוּ / וְלֹא־מַרְאֶה וְנֶחְמְדֵהוּ׃$$

However, the divisions marked by the masoretic accents is quite different. In the Hebrew text *Athnach*, one of the major

---

[4] Cohen, "Masoretic Accents as a Biblical Commentary," 9–10.

120 *The Exegetical Roles of the Divisions*

delimiters, occurs between וְלֹא הָדָר and וְנִרְאֵהוּ. In addition, there is a *Tiphcha* between וְלֹא־מַרְאֶה and וְנֶחְמְדֵהוּ even though it is a final disjunctive. We should therefore translate this passage as follows:

> He grew up before him like a tender shoot, /
> and like a root out of dry land. /
> He had no beauty or majesty. //
> Let us look at him although he has no charm. Let us desire him.

Here, the masoretic accentuation seems to create a contrast with Isaiah 44:9, which also uses the same two main verbs (חמד and ראה), but instead focuses on the vanity of idol worship ("Those who fashion a graven image are all of them futile, and their *precious* things are of no profit; even their own witnesses fail to *see* or know, so that they will be put to shame.") (Isaiah 44:9 [NAS]).

8.2 Emphasizing Certain Words or Phrases

Having explored how the masoretic accents can resolve textual ambiguity, we turn now to a second way they aid us in exegesis: by emphasizing certain words or phrases. Since the divisions by Hebrew accents follow prosodic structure, they mark the mental representation of a spoken sentence hierarchically characterized as perceived in speech.[5] The result is that the accentual divisions place certain significant words or phrases in particular positions and thereby emphasize them. We now look at several examples of the accents' function.

The following set of passages illustrate the typical accentuation and relationship of two words in a construct chain. As these examples demonstrate, the two words in the construct chain are normally connected by a conjunctive accent because they are syntactically and semantically close.

---

[5] Nespor and Vogel, *Prosodic Phonology*, 1–3.

8.2 Emphasizing Certain Words or Phrases   121

Exodus 12:43,

זֹאת / חֻקַּת הַפָּסַח

Numbers 4:4,

זֹאת / עֲבֹדַת בְּנֵי־קְהָת

Numbers 7:84,

זֹאת ׀/ חֲנֻכַּת הַמִּזְבֵּחַ

Numbers 19:2,

זֹאת / חֻקַּת הַתּוֹרָה

However, there are exceptions to this general rule. In the book of Leviticus, the expression זאת תורת functions as a formula to introduce certain ritual and legal practices. In this context, the most significant word appears right after this formula in order to differentiate one law from another. Thus, a pause stands before the expression, breaking the construct chain.[6]

Leviticus 6:2,

זֹאת תּוֹרַת / הָעֹלָה

Leviticus 6:7,

וְזֹאת תּוֹרַת / הַמִּנְחָה

Leviticus 12:7,

זֹאת תּוֹרַת / הַיֹּלֶדֶת

Leviticus 15:32,

זֹאת תּוֹרַת / הַזָּב

Sometimes unusual divisions draw special attention to certain words or phrases. Consider the following three examples from Genesis 1:21, 28:16, and Daniel 6:12.

The accentual divisions found in Genesis 1:21 are odd. It would be better to place the major break between כָּנָף לְמִינֵהוּ and וַיִּרְא אֱלֹהִים in order to divide the two sentences syntactically. However, the major disjunctive *Athnach* appears in the phrase אֶת־הַתַּנִּינִם הַגְּדֹלִים, which draws attention to the matchless nature of these creatures in comparison to other creatures. The emphasis the accents place on these creatures is reflected in the attention that Jewish fables give to them.[7]

---

[6] Cohen, *The System of Accentuation in the Hebrew Bible*, 28–29.

[7] Wickes (*Accentuation of the Twenty-One*, 33–34), thought that this kind of reading related to the Jewish Haggadic teaching.

וַיִּבְרָא אֱלֹהִים /

אֶת־הַתַּנִּינִם הַגְּדֹלִים //

וְאֵת כָּל־נֶפֶשׁ הַחַיָּה | הָרֹמֶשֶׂת אֲשֶׁר שָׁרְצוּ הַמַּיִם לְמִינֵהֶם /

וְאֵת כָּל־עוֹף כָּנָף לְמִינֵהוּ /

וַיַּרְא אֱלֹהִים כִּי־טוֹב:

God created /
the sea monsters, GIGANTIC ones! //
and every living thing that creeps, which the waters teemed
after their kind, /
and every winged bird after its kind; /
and God saw that it was good.

In Genesis 28:16, at first glance the placement of a main
break in the middle of the direct speech seems awkward
because the phrase introducing direct speech usually takes
the main pause. However, sometimes the direct speech is
interrupted by the main pause to emphasize the most mean-
ingful portion of the direct speech. This certainly seems to be
the case in Genesis 28:16:

וַיֹּאמֶר אָכֵן יֵשׁ יְהוָה /

בַּמָּקוֹם הַזֶּה //

וְאָנֹכִי לֹא יָדָעְתִּי:

Then he said, "Surely the LORD is /
in THIS VERY PLACE."//
"I surely did not know it."

The major break in the first half stands before the phrase
בַּמָּקוֹם הַזֶּה, and this phrase itself holds *Athnach*. This phrase

8.2 Emphasizing Certain Words or Phrases 123

is the center point of Jacob's speech. This draws attention to the fact that the Lord's presence was in "THIS very place" where Jacob slept!

In Daniel 6:12, we would expect the main break to appear between הַרְגִּשׁוּ and וְהַשְׁכַּחוּ, but it instead occurs right after לְדָנִיֵּאל. The purpose of this is to highlight the person of "Daniel," who is making a petition, asking his God for help against the king's solemn decree to prohibit everyone from praying to other gods.[8]

אֱדַיִן גֻּבְרַיָּא אִלֵּךְ הַרְגִּשׁוּ /
וְהַשְׁכַּחוּ לְדָנִיֵּאל //
בָּעֵא וּמִתְחַנַּן קֳדָם אֱלָהֵהּ:

Then these men rushed together /
and found (after a little pause) DANIEL //
making petition and asking his God for help.

Similarly, the Hebrew Bible contains some instances in which the major pause comes right before short phrases or sentences in order to emphasize them in the final position of a whole verse. A good example of this comes from Genesis 38:6-7:

וַיִּקַּח יְהוּדָה אִשָּׁה לְעֵר בְּכוֹרוֹ //
וּשְׁמָהּ תָּמָר: /

וַיְהִי עֵר בְּכוֹר יְהוּדָה /
רַע בְּעֵינֵי יְהוָה //
וַיְמִתֵהוּ יְהוָה:

---

[8] Wickes, *Accentuation of the Twenty-One*, 34.

124   *The Exegetical Roles of the Divisions*

Now Judah got a wife for Er, his first-born, //
Now her name was Tamar.

But Er, Judah's first-born, /
was evil in the sight of the LORD, //
so the LORD put him to death.

In Genesis 38:6 the placement of *Athnach* prior to
וּשְׁמָהּ תָּמָר, rather than after it as would be expected, emphasizes the verse's second half ("Now her name was Tamar").
The purpose of this is to introduce Tamar, a new main
character in the narrative, who will figure significantly in a
shocking episode later in the story. The emphasis placed on
Tamar thus creates foreshadowing as a literary device. The
next verse similarly stresses the second half, "so the LORD
put him to death," to point out the horrendous result of Er's
evil deeds.

Sometimes the main break appears in the introductory
part of a verse in order to draw attention to some features
announced in the introduction. Genesis 35:10 illustrates this
phenomenon well:

$$\text{וַיֹּאמֶר־לֹו אֱלֹהִים שִׁמְךָ יַעֲקֹב //}$$

$$\text{לֹא־יִקָּרֵא שִׁמְךָ עֹוד יַעֲקֹב /}$$

$$\text{כִּי אִם־יִשְׂרָאֵל יִהְיֶה שְׁמֶךָ /}$$

$$\text{וַיִּקְרָא אֶת־שְׁמֹו יִשְׂרָאֵל׃}$$

God said to him, "Your name is Jacob; //
Your name shall not be called Jacob, /
But Israel shall be your name." /
Thus, he called his name Israel.

Genesis 35:10 exhibits a well-balanced parallelistic structure,
chiastically repeating יַעֲקֹב, יִשְׂרָאֵל, and שֵׁם with two different
suffixes. The major break emphasizes the fact that although
he is presently named Jacob, no longer will his name be

8.3 Creating Dramatic Effect in Biblical Narrative

Jacob. Rather, his name will be Israel, which establishes a new identity for Jacob and his descendants. Jacob's new name Israel is also highlighted by its placement with *Silluq*.

8.3 Creating Dramatic Effect in Biblical Narrative

Finally, in addition to clarifying ambiguous meanings and emphasizing certain words or phrases, the masoretic accents can contribute to the dramatic effect of biblical narrative. Since the accentual divisions are based on prosodic structure in a real utterance, they reflect pauses that create dramatic effect, especially in biblical narrative. The accents do this primarily in two ways: by representing quick actions without interruption and by skipping over less important details of the narrative.

Let us first consider examples that show how the accents can represent quick actions. When a series of verbs appears without many interruptions or major accentual divisions, those verbs usually describe a character's quick, successive actions. The idea here is that the fewer the interruptions, the quicker the actions. Genesis 38:13–14 provides a good example of this:

וַיֻּגַּד לְתָמָר לֵאמֹר //

הִנֵּה חָמִיךְ עֹלֶה תִמְנָתָה לָגֹז צֹאנוֹ: /

וַתָּסַר בִּגְדֵי אַלְמְנוּתָהּ מֵעָלֶיהָ /

וַתְּכַס בַּצָּעִיף וַתִּתְעַלָּף /

וַתֵּשֶׁב בְּפֶתַח עֵינַיִם /

אֲשֶׁר עַל־דֶּרֶךְ תִּמְנָתָה //

כִּי רָאֲתָה כִּי־גָדַל שֵׁלָה /

וְהִוא לֹא־נִתְּנָה לוֹ לְאִשָּׁה:

The Exegetical Roles of the Divisions

And it was told to Tamar, saying, //
"Hey, your father-in-law is now going up to Timnah to
shear his sheep."

So she removed her widow's garments from her /
and covered herself with a veil, and wrapped herself, /
and sat in the gateway of Enaim, //
which is on the road to Timnah; /
for she saw that Shelah grew up, /
but she was not given to him as a wife.

When Tamar heard that Judah was going up to Timnah, she moved quickly and strategically. Her quick actions contrast with her past of long-waiting and add to the dramatic effect of the narrative by emphasizing Tamar's haste to put her plan into action.

Another example of the accents' use to depict quick, successive actions comes from Genesis 25:34. This verse describes Esau's acts of eating, drinking, rising, and going away as if they are just one action. Such quick actions may reflect how hungry Esau was, but the Bible explains that Esau moved quickly because he despised his birthright. Esau did not consider his birthright to be anything beneficial, instead treating it as less valuable than bread and lentil stew.

וְיַעֲקֹב נָתַן לְעֵשָׂו /

לֶחֶם וּנְזִיד עֲדָשִׁים /

וַיֹּאכַל וַיֵּשְׁתְּ /

וַיָּקָם וַיֵּלַךְ //

וַיִּבֶז עֵשָׂו אֶת־הַבְּכֹרָה׃

Then Jacob gave Esau /
bread and lentil stew; /
and he ate, drank,/
rose, went away //
(why?) because Esau despised his birthright.

8.3 Creating Dramatic Effect in Biblical Narrative

Similarly, 1 Samuel 19:12 describes David's speedy actions of fleeing as if they were one motion. The last phrase of the first half ("through a window") reflects David's urgency to escape imminent danger because people normally leave a building through the door, not through a window.

וַתֹּרֶד מִיכַל אֶת־דָּוִד בְּעַד הַחַלּוֹן //

וַיֵּלֶךְ וַיִּבְרַח וַיִּמָּלֵט:

When Michal let David down through a window, //
he went out, fled, escaped.

Jonah 1:2–3 depicts a contrast between God's urgent command to go to Nineveh and Jonah's scurrying escape to Tarshish. This contrast is especially highlighted by v. 3. In v. 3, the repetition of a phrase (מִלִּפְנֵי יְהוָה) emphasizes Jonah's intentional fleeing from the Lord with a main break marked by *Athnach* and *Silluq*. The first verbal phrase of the first half of the verse (וַיָּקָם) provides the general description of Jonah's escape, while the verbal phrases of the second half (וַיֵּרֶד... וַיִּמְצָא... וַיִּתֵּן... וַיֵּרֶד) offer the specific description of his flight through a series of action verbs.

קוּם לֵךְ אֶל־נִינְוֵה הָעִיר הַגְּדוֹלָה וּקְרָא עָלֶיהָ //

כִּי־עָלְתָה רָעָתָם לְפָנָי:

וַיָּקָם יוֹנָה לִבְרֹחַ תַּרְשִׁישָׁה /

מִלִּפְנֵי יְהוָה //

וַיֵּרֶד יָפוֹ וַיִּמְצָא אָנִיָּה | בָּאָה תַרְשִׁישׁ /

וַיִּתֵּן שְׂכָרָהּ וַיֵּרֶד בָּהּ לָבוֹא עִמָּהֶם תַּרְשִׁישָׁה /

מִלִּפְנֵי יְהוָה:

"Rise, go to Nineveh the great city, and preach against it, //

128   *The Exegetical Roles of the Divisions*

for their wickedness has come up before Me."
But Jonah rose up to flee to Tarshish /
from the presence of the LORD. //
He went down to Joppa, found a ship going to Tarshish, /
paid the fare, and went down to her to go with them to
Tarshish /
from the presence of the LORD.

Here, it is helpful to examine a biblical verse that also
seemingly represents quick action, but actually does not.
Consider, for example, Judges 3:21.

$$\text{וַיִּשְׁלַח אֵהוּד אֶת־יַד שְׂמֹאלוֹ /}$$

$$\text{וַיִּקַּח אֶת־הַחֶרֶב /}$$

$$\text{מֵעַל יֶרֶךְ יְמִינוֹ //}$$

$$\text{וַיִּתְקָעֶהָ בְּבִטְנוֹ:}$$

Ehud stretched out his left hand, /
grabbed the sword /
from his right thigh up //
and thrust it into his belly.

Judges 3:21 depicts the actions by which Ehud killed the
king Eglon. But, instead of representing Ehud's actions as fast
and successive actions, the narrative portrays them slowly in
detail. It does so through its use of many phrasal interruptions between verbs, which results in more words between
accentual pauses. Ehud does not merely stretch out his hand
and grab the sword; rather, he stretches out his left hand and
pulls his sword up from his right thigh. It is worth noting that
the word שְׂמֹאלוֹ ("left") appears for the first time in this
narrative. In Judges 3:15, Ehud's left-handedness is indirectly
expressed by the phrase אִישׁ אִטֵּר יַד־יְמִינוֹ (lit., "a man restrict-
ing the use of his right hand"). The narrative emphasizes
"right" until it reaches v. 21; Ehud was the Benjamite
(בֶּן־הַיְמִינִי; lit., "son of right hand") in v. 15 and placed his

8.3 Creating Dramatic Effect in Biblical Narrative 129

sword on his right thigh (עַל־יֶרֶךְ יְמִינוֹ) in v. 16. However, v. 21 describes Ehud's left hand as the hand used for killing his long-standing enemy.

The second half of Judges 3:21 concludes Ehud's final fatal attack: he thrusts the sword deeply into the belly of the king Eglon. Thus, Judges 3:21 resembles a slow-motion action scene in a movie. The camera focuses on Ehud's actions and slowly follows the flow of his left hand holding the sword until he carries out his goal.

In addition to representing successive actions quickly, the accents can also contribute to the dramatic effect of a narrative by encouraging the reader to read general information quickly in order to get to the most important details. This occurs when an accentual division, especially one in the domain of *Rebia*, is quite long. To say that its length is "long" means that several conjunctive accents appear consecutively. According to the simplification rule, disjunctives are replaced by conjunctives when the distance between disjunctives is too close to read them naturally. Removing less important disjunctives (such as those at the D3 level) therefore promotes fast and natural reading of the insignificant parts of a verse, as illustrated by 1 Samuel 25:39 and Genesis 21:14.

In 1 Samuel 25:39, David praises God for judging his case of reproach from Nabal:

וַיִּשְׁמַ֤ע דָּוִד֙ כִּ֣י מֵ֣ת נָבָ֔ל /

וַיֹּ֡אמֶר בָּר֣וּךְ יְהוָ֡ה אֲשֶׁ֣ר רָב֩ אֶת־רִ֨יב חֶרְפָּתִ֤י מִיַּ֣ד נָבָ֔ל /

וְאֶת־עַבְדּוֹ֙ חָשַׂ֣ךְ מֵֽרָעָ֔ה /

וְאֵת֙ רָעַ֣ת נָבָ֔ל /

הֵשִׁ֥יב יְהוָ֖ה בְּרֹאשׁ֑וֹ //

וַיִּשְׁלַ֤ח דָּוִד֙ וַיְדַבֵּ֣ר בַּאֲבִיגַ֔יִל /

לְקַחְתָּ֖הּ ל֥וֹ לְאִשָּֽׁה:

130   *The Exegetical Roles of the Divisions*

> When David heard that Nabal was dead, /
> he said, "Blessed be the LORD, who has judged the case of
> my reproach from the hand of Nabal, /
> and has protected his servant from evil. /
> the evildoing of Nabal /
> The LORD has paid on his own head." //
> Then David sent, talked with Abigail, /
> to take her as his wife.

Here, the first line of the relatively short first half (וַיִּשְׁמַע דָּוִד כִּי מֵת נָבָל) is divided by *Segolta* because this disjunctive replaces *Little Zaqeph*, one of the main delimiters. This line sets the stage for the event that occurs after Nabal was dead. In contrast, the second line of the first half, which is governed by *Rebia*, is quite long, consisting of five conjunctives and four disjunctives (וַיֹּאמֶר בָּרוּךְ יְהוָה אֲשֶׁר רָב אֶת־רִיב חֶרְפָּתִי מִיַּד נָבָל). The information provided in the second line is therefore of little importance: the focus of the verse is not on David's prayer, but on the fact that Nabal was dead; the first and fifth lines of the verse's first half are positioned like an inclusio structure ("Nabal was dead" vs. "The LORD has paid on his own head"). Interestingly, the second half of the verse reveals David's true intention. It recounts his quick actions after hearing that Nabal was dead, namely sending his servants to Abigail and asking her to be his wife.[9]

Another example of skipping over general information not so important to the narrative is found in Genesis 21:14. Here, Abraham prepares bread and water for Hagar and sends her away.

---

[9] Notably, Abigail also responds quickly just a few verses later in the narrative (1 Sam. 25:42).

8.4 Summary

וַיַּשְׁכֵּם אַבְרָהָם | בַּבֹּקֶר וַיִּקַּח־לֶחֶם וְחֵמַת מַיִם וַיִּתֵּן אֶל־
הָגָר שָׂם עַל־שִׁכְמָהּ וְאֶת־הַיֶּלֶד וַיְשַׁלְּחֶהָ //

וַתֵּלֶךְ וַתֵּתַע /

בְּמִדְבַּר בְּאֵר שָׁבַע:

Abraham rose early in the morning, and took bread and a
skin of water,
and gave to Hagar, putting on her shoulder, as well as the
boy,
and sent her away. //
She departed, wandered around /
in the wilderness of Beersheba.

The description of Abraham's deeds is long, but it does not
add any significant information because – as the accents
reveal – the main point of the verse is to say that Abraham
sent Hagar away and that as a result she departed and
wandered in the wilderness. By quickly skipping over certain
information to recount its main point, this verse foreshadows
Hagar's impending suffering in the wilderness.

8.4 Summary

In this chapter, we explored three important roles of the
Hebrew accents: clarifying ambiguous meanings, emphasizing certain words or phrases, and creating dramatic effect in
biblical narrative. The examples provided demonstrate
clearly that the masoretic accents can have significant bearing
on the exegesis of the biblical text. By paying close attention
to the accentual divisions of the text, our understanding of
the biblical text is enhanced and we can attain insights that
Hebrew syntax alone may not provide.

Appendix A

The Functional Development of the Tiberian Hebrew Accents[1]

There are two systems of accentuation in the Tiberian manuscripts of the Hebrew Bible: one used in the "Twenty-One Books" and another used in the "Three Books" (Psalms, Proverbs, and Job, excluding the narrative portion of Job 1:1–3:1 and 42:7–17]). The present book focuses on the former, simpler system, although both systems are functionally the same in terms of the issues discussed here.[2]

Concerning the functions of the Tiberian accentuation system, nearly all scholars agree that the accents serve to mark at least three distinctive things: (1) stress, (2) musical notations, and (3) punctuation markers.[3] Let us now examine these three purposes, with the goal of determining the primary and original function of the accents.

The first purpose of the Tiberian accentuation system is to indicate stress. To do so, the accent is usually placed over or under the main stressed syllable of each word. As in many

---

[1] This is an abridged version of my article originally published in *Hebrew Studies*. Park, "Pointing to the Accents in the Scroll," 73–88.

[2] For the accent system of the "Three Books," see Appendix C.

[3] Wickes, *Accentuation of the Twenty-One*, 1–2; Breuer, טעמי המקרא בכ"א ספרים ובספרי אמ"ת, 3–9; Yeivin, *Introduction to the Tiberian Masorah*, 178; Dresher, "Tiberian Hebrew System of Accents," 5–6; Aronoff, "Orthography and Linguistic Theory," 32–36; Weil, *The Masoretic Chant of the Bible*, 4; Weisberg, "The Rare Accents of the Twenty-One Books," 317; Janis, "A Grammar of the Biblical Accents," 3–6; Dotan, "Prolegomenon-Research in Biblical Accentuation," vii–viii.

134   *Appendix A Functional Development of Hebrew Accents*

other languages, stress in the Tiberian accentuation system is phonemic; that is, the meaning of a word can change depending on which syllable is stressed.[4] Consider the following examples:

Genesis 37:8

וַיֹּאמְרוּ לוֹ אֶחָיו הֲמָלֹךְ תִּמְלֹךְ עָלֵינוּ
אִם־מָשׁוֹל תִּמְשֹׁל בָּנוּ

His brothers said to him, "Will you really rule over us?
Or will you truly reign over us?"

Genesis 11:5

וְאֶת־הַמִּגְדָּל אֲשֶׁר בָּנוּ בְּנֵי הָאָדָם׃

The tower that men had built

Genesis 15:17

וַיְהִי הַשֶּׁמֶשׁ בָּאָה

When the sun had set,

Genesis 29:6

וְהִנֵּה רָחֵל בִּתּוֹ בָּאָה

Look, Rachel his daughter is coming.

Since the position of the stress is phonologically significant in Biblical Hebrew, it is reasonable to suppose that marking its position would be an important role for any diacritical system. Marking stress, however, cannot be considered the primary function of the Tiberian accentuation system because, if this

---

[4] Blau, *A Grammar of Biblical Hebrew*, 19.

Appendix A Functional Development of Hebrew Accents   135

were the only function, the Masoretes would not have needed so many different accents. Furthermore, accents for indicating stress over each word cannot be found in the early stage of the Babylonian Masorah or the Proto-Palestinian Masorah.[5] In fact, even in the Tiberian system, some postpositive or prepositive accents like *Segolta, Zarqa,* and *Yethib* are not marked over or under the stressed syllables.

These observations lead E. Werner to suggest that the use of the accents to mark stress is a later development.[6] However, this suggestion faces at least two difficulties. On the one hand, some Palestinian manuscripts show more detailed features of conjunctives than the Tiberian system but do not place their accents upon stressed syllables.[7] This indicates that marking stress positions was not the primary concern of the Palestinian accentual signs.[8] On the other hand, marking accents over stressed syllables is attested in some early Babylonian manuscripts.[9] Therefore, the function of marking stress should not be considered a later development.

Although we have no documented evidence regarding the existence of stress in Biblical Hebrew, various phenomena reflecting stress positioning can be reasonably postulated in it. Stress must have existed during the biblical period because stress is a suprasegmental quality innate to a word in a language, and therefore its existence is more ancient than any other phonological phenomena in Biblical Hebrew.[10] The question, then, is why this function is not marked much until the later masoretic tradition. The reason for this might be that the Masoretes did not feel any urgent need to mark the

---

[5] Dotan, "Masorah," 637; Morag, "מפעלם של ראשונים: על דרכם של חכמי המסורה ועל מונחים ארמיים שטבעו," 49–77.

[6] Werner, *The Sacred Bridge*, 413.

[7] Revell, "Hebrew Accents and Greek Ekphonetic Neumes," 148.

[8] Revell, "Hebrew Accents and Greek Ekphonetic Neumes," 148.

[9] Shoshany, "בחינה מחודשת של המתאם בהתפתחות מערות הניקוד וטעמי המקרא במסורת הבבלית," 251–267.

[10] It is beyond the shadow of a doubt that vowels and consonants in a word are the most fundamental phonological entities.

136   *Appendix A Functional Development of Hebrew Accents*

stressed syllable because the text's readers already knew where to put the stress. Regardless, it is almost certain that marking stress was not the major reason why the Tiberian accentuation system was developed.

The second and third functions for the masoretic accents are to provide musical notation and mark punctuation, respectively. Although scholars debate which of these two is primary, most tend to believe that the former is original for several reasons.

First, the cantillation of biblical texts guided by the Tiberian accentuation system is practiced in synagogues to this day.[11] Wickes comments, "The Hebrew accentuation is essentially a musical system. The accents are musical signs – originally designed to represent and preserve a particular mode of cantillation or musical declamation, which was in use for the public reading of the Old Testament text at the time of their introduction, and which had been handed down by tradition from much earlier times."[12]

Second, the accents' musical function may be also supported by the Talmud. In *b. Megillah* 32a,

> R. Shefatiah further said in the name of R. Johanan, "As for one who reads (the Scripture) without *melody* and studies (the Mishnah) without *a tune*, the Scripture says, 'Wherefore I gave them also statutes that were not good, etc.' (Ezek. 20:25)."

Also, in *b. Berakoth* 62a,

> Why should one not wipe with the right hand but with the left? Raba said, "Because the Torah was given with the right hand, as it is written, 'At His right hand was a fiery law unto them.' (Deut. 33:2)" Rabbah b. Hanah said, "Because it is brought to the mouth." R. Simeon b. Lakish said, "Because one binds the tefillin

---

[11] Yeivin, *Introduction to the Tiberian Masorah*, 178; Breuer, טעמי המקרא בכ"א ובספרי אמ"ת, 3–9; Weil, *The Masoretic Chant of the Bible*, 4; Revell, "Masoretic Accent," 594–596, and "Hebrew Accents and Greek Ekphonetic Neumes," 141–142.

[12] Wickes, *Accentuation of the Twenty-One*, 1–2.

Appendix A Functional Development of Hebrew Accents   137

(on the left arm) with it." R. Nahman b. Isaac said, "Because one points to *the accents* in the scroll with it. Similarly, R. Eliezer says, "Because one eats with it." R. Joshua says, "Because one writes with it." R. Akiba says, "Because one points with it (right hand) to *the accents* in the scroll."

Rashi thought that the term טעמי תורה "the accents of the Torah" referred to "the cantillation of Scripture," with corresponding movements made with the right hand according to the musical accents, because it was prohibited to use an accentuated scroll for public reading. Furthermore, he mentioned that the Palestinian readers of his day (the late eleventh century) practiced cheironomy when learning Scripture.[13]

This brings us to the third consideration, based not on extra-biblical tradition but on internal evidence. If punctuation was the primary function of the accents, it is unclear why the Masoretes needed so many of them.[14] The existence of numerous disjunctives would still be understandable due to their hierarchical and distributive characteristics. However, since there is no hierarchical relationship among the conjunctives, their existence can only be explained in terms of musical value. In particular, according to the rules of dichotomy, some disjunctives appear in combinations only with certain conjunctives.[15] For example, the conjunctive *Munach* plays a role as the first servus of *Rebia*, always being followed by it.[16] Thus, Wickes comments, "This *formal* dichotomy necessarily supplied (as far as it went) the basis

---

[13] As Werner rightly proposed, cheironomy was a very important ancient practice, especially in the religious and cultic setting of Egypt, Mesopotamia, and ancient Greece. Werner, *The Sacred Bridge*, 107–109. For cheironomy, see Herzog, "Masoretic Accents (Musical Rendition)," 656–664.

[14] Breuer, טעמי המקרא בכ"א ספרים ובספרי אמ"ת, 20.

[15] Price, *The Syntax of Masoretic Accents in the Hebrew Bible*, 19–52; Yeivin, *Introduction to the Tiberian Masorah*, 176–218; Wickes, *Accentuation of the Twenty-One*, 29–129.

[16] Yeivin, *Introduction to the Tiberian Masorah*, 192–193; Wickes, *Accentuation of the Twenty-One*, 97–98. See the detailed discussion about conjunctive accents in Chapter 5.

138   *Appendix A Functional Development of Hebrew Accents*

for the *musical,* and from its constant recurrence seems to have suggested to the originators of the accentual system a guiding principle for the musical divisions *in general.*[17] Similarly, Revell contends that the different combinations among the accents may relate to "the music of several different forms of chant," calling groups of accents "motifs or tropes."[18] This argument based on internal evidence is the most convincing regarding the musical function of the accents.

Compelling as they may seem, the first two considerations based on Jewish tradition are not entirely adequate because some other Talmudic passages may support a punctuational function for the accents. According to *b. Nedarim* 37b,

> As for one who maintains that payment is for the teaching of accentuation, why does he reject the view that it is for acting as guardian? He reasons: Do daughters then need guarding? Then, as for one who maintains that the fee is for guardianship, why does he reject the view that it is for teaching accents? He holds that accents are also biblical. For R. Ika b. Abin said in the name of R. Hananel in Rab's name, "What is the meaning of 'And they read in the book, in the law of God, distinctly, and they gave the sense, so that they understood the reading' (Neh. 8:8)"? They read in the book, it, the law of God, refers to Scripture; "distinctly," to Targum; *"and they gave the sense," to the division of sentences; "so that they understood the reading," to the accentuation;* others say, to the masoroth.

Likewise, in *b. Chagigah* 6b (= *b. Yoma* 52b),

> "How is this verse to be understood, 'And he sent the young men of the children of Israel, who offered burnt offerings of lambs, and sacrificed peace offerings of oxen unto the LORD' (Exod. 24:5)? Or perhaps both were oxen? What difference does it make?" Mar Zutra said, "In regard to *the punctuation.*" R. Abba,

---

[17] Wickes, *Accentuation of the Twenty-One,* 29–30, 80 (italics his). The law of substitution in the accentuation system also supports the musical purpose of the accents. See Price, *The Syntax of Masoretic Accents in the Hebrew Bible,* 31–32, 154–155.

[18] Revell, "Masoretic Accents," 594.

Appendix A Functional Development of Hebrew Accents   139

the son of Raba, said, "In regard to one who says, 'I vow [to offer] a burnt-offering like the burnt-offering which Israel offered in the wilderness.'" What [must he offer]? Were they oxen or lambs? It remains [undecided].

R. Hisda's question is, apparently, whether Exodus 24:5 should be understood as saying that both burnt offerings and peace offerings ordered by Moses consisted of oxen. In response, Mar Zutra points to the accent *Athnach* on the word עֹלֹת, interpreting it as a punctuation mark that indicates the end of a sentence, and that consequently the reference to oxen after this sign does not necessarily apply to burnt offerings mentioned before it. R. Hisda's addition of the word כבשים "sheep" to the first half of the verse (where the Masoretic text reads וַיִּשְׁלַח אֶת־נַעֲרֵי בְּנֵי יִשְׂרָאֵל וַיַּעֲלוּ עֹלֹת וַיִּזְבְּחוּ זְבָחִים שְׁלָמִים לַיהוָה פָּרִים:) is therefore justified.[19]

How, then, do we determine the primary function of the accents in the masoretic system? Was it punctuational for recitation or musical for song? Admittedly, choosing between the two is a difficult task because the Tiberian accentuation system clearly indicates its musical elements by means of various kinds of conjunctives and patterned accent combinations, while also designating its punctuational elements by means of the pausal duration pattern. We must ask whether it served these two functions concurrently or consecutively?

Here, it is worthwhile to turn our attention to the empirical insight, observed by modern cognitive theorists, that there are no apparent differences between intonation patterns of normal speech and musical melodies except for some relatively minor factors, such as duration.[20] According to this research, it would not be surprising if the masoretic accents

---

[19] Tov, *Textual Criticism*, 69.

[20] Patel, *Music, Language, and the Brain*, especially chapters 3–5; Ross, Choi, and Purves, "Musical Intervals in Speech," 9852–9857; Bowling, Gill, Choi, Prinz, and Purves, "Major and Minor Music Compared to Excited and Subdued Speech," 491–503; Dresher, "Between Music and Speech," 43–58.

140   *Appendix A Functional Development of Hebrew Accents*

were both punctuational (in their distribution of pauses for normal speech) and musical (in their various combinations to produce music motifs). The two functions likely coexisted in the masoretic accentuation system.

With this discussion in mind, is it possible to determine which of this system's two functions was the first to develop? Werner suggests that as a norm, punctuation emerges earlier than musical notation in many languages.[21] The question is, however, whether this generalization applies to the Tiberian accentuation system. Several considerations help us answer this question. To begin with, there are at least three good reasons to believe that a development from major disjunctive accents to conjunctives within the Tiberian accentuation system took place in several stages.

The first reason is Revell's observation that the distribution of spacings in Rylands Greek Papyrus 458, one of the oldest Septuagint manuscripts, is identical to that of some major disjunctive accents in the masoretic Bible.[22] Since Papyrus 458 is dated to the second century BCE, the colometric tradition concerning major disjunctives must be relatively old.

Second, conjunctives were originally not counted in ancient tradition among טעמים ("accents") since they appear with words in phrases as connectors to the following disjunctives.[23] They were not initially categorized as accents and only later came to be treated as such because they bear relatively weak stresses as connectors between dominant disjunctive accents.

Third, there were no conjunctives in the earlier Babylonian tradition, whose accentuation system bears better witness than the Tiberian one to the initial stages of the

---

[21] Werner, *Sacred Bridge*, 104.

[22] Revell, "The Oldest Evidence for the Hebrew Accent System," 214–222, "Biblical Punctuation and Chant in the Second Temple Period," 181–198, "Pausal Forms in Biblical Hebrew," 165–179, and "Pausal Forms and the Structure of Biblical Poetry," 186–199.

[23] Breuer, פיסוק טעמים שבמקרא, 58.

Appendix A Functional Development of Hebrew Accents 141

accents' development. Of course, lack of conjunctives in relatively early sources does not definitively prove that these signs did not exist at that time. However, the three arguments that have just been outlined do reasonably indicate the functional primacy of major disjunctives over conjunctives, probably signifying that the former was the first to emerge. Here it is important to mention that this applies only to major disjunctives because some rare accents like *Shalsheleth* and *Great Pazer* were certainly added much later by medieval Jewish communities. It is apparent, therefore, that the Tiberian accentuation system did not emerge in its final shape at once but rather developed in stages over time. It represents a mixture of practices, some of which reflect ancient traditions and others that were developed by the Masoretes for their own exegetical purposes. Although it is difficult to separate the two elements, the punctuational function of the disjunctive accents should be considered the most ancient, probably of earlier provenance than conjunctives.

Furthermore, the masoretic accents were not musical notes but rather musical neumes. Werner explains the differences between a neume and a note, as follows: "The basic distinction between a neume and a note is that: the former usually stands not for a single note, but for a whole phrase, whereas modern notation has one sign for each individual note. Not all early neumes, and none of the ecphonetic systems can be transcribed in modern notation without the help of oral tradition."[24] In most cases, synagogue and church practices display a trend of gradual transition from ecphonetic accents to a more exact musical notation.[25] The standard Tiberian accentuation system, with its various combinations of the accents (i.e., neumes), made it possible for ancient readers to chant the biblical texts with ambiguous directions of upward or downward voice movement in accord

[24] Werner, *Sacred Bridge*, 105.
[25] Werner, *Sacred Bridge*, 104; Treitler, "Reading and Singing," 135–208.

142   *Appendix A Functional Development of Hebrew Accents*

with an orally transmitted tradition. However, that is not the same as singing these texts because chanting was in fact a form of speech marked by cadential formulas.[26]

Finally, since the masoretic accents are not musical notes, there is no way to use them to write down rhythmic flow or temporal periodicity of music in the text. This implies that the Tiberian accentuation system could have developed over time from the punctuational purpose for recitation to the musical purpose for singing.

To be sure, these considerations do not preclude the possibility that musical realization existed from the outset, supported by an orally transmitted tradition. However, there is no documentary evidence for such a tradition, and in the Tiberian accentuation system we can trace only two major functional elements: punctuation for recitation and cantillation for chanting with melodic formulas (originated by neumes), yet not for singing. Therefore, it appears likely that the Tiberian accentuation system functionally developed from punctuation to cantillation. That is why we observe these two functional elements coexisting in this system.

In conclusion, it is evident that marking stressed syllables was a secondary function of the Tiberian accentuation system. The punctuational function of the accents for recitation probably gave rise to other relational divisions of a unit. Finally, the accents came to be used for cantillation in addition to punctuation, although this development did not bring about a full-fledged system of musical notation.

---

[26] Treitler, "Reading and Singing," 179.

Appendix B

Three Accentuation Systems within the Masoretic Tradition[1]

There are three masoretic traditions: Babylonian, Palestinian, and Tiberian. Each of them has different graphemes for the vowel and accent signs. The Tiberian accentuation system was the latest development among the masoretic traditions because of its most comprehensive and sophisticated system of vocalization and accentuation. The early Babylonian and Palestinian texts neither possessed conjunctive accents nor did they mark accents upon stressed syllables; they instead marked accents only upon words. Moreover, the Palestinian tradition displayed two different accentuation systems (prose and poetic) like the Tiberian, whereas the Babylonian tradition used only one accentuation system in all books.[2]

W. Wickes believes that the Palestinian tradition presented the most primitive accentuation pattern. He comments,

> we may conclude, with absolute certainty, from the instances cited, that the Palestinian punctuation was before the originators of this superlinear system (i.e., Babylonian system). Their attempt, however, to modify and improve upon it must, as

---

[1] This section is taken partially from my book, *Typology in Biblical Hebrew Meter*, 45–49.

[2] Yeivin, *Introduction to the Tiberian Masorah*, 158, 165; Dotan, "Masorah," 624–642.

144 *Appendix B Three Accentuation Systems*

far at least as the accents are concerned, be pronounced a failure, and for us quite worthless. Inconsequent and contradictory, this new system is a mere travesty of the Palestinian.[3]

However, E. Revell proposes on the basis of his research on the Palestinian texts that the various written accent signs in the Palestinian tradition reflected a variety of communities within the "Western" system (which also included the Tiberian system) and that the two systems (Palestinian and Tiberian) were "different ways of indicating the same basic phenomena, used in different communities at the same time."[4] As argued by Revell, less homogeneously written graphemes in the Palestinian system do not prove any primitiveness. Rather, their seeming primitiveness is in fact a mark of sophistication, a conclusion supported by the fact that several Palestinian manuscripts present greater details of features of conjunctives than the Tiberian system.[5] Revell further suggests that the Palestinian accent signs were not intended to mark stress position. He states, "the difference between the Palestinian and Tiberian traditions is, at base, one of writing systems only; that the Palestinian and the Tiberian pointing systems were not used to represent basically different reading traditions, but that both were used for a variety of forms of a single 'Western' stream of tradition."[6] Revell's argument is coherent and convincing because the

---

[3] Wickes, *Accentuation of the Twenty-One*, 149–150. He states, "I believe that it would be equally easy to shew [show] that the superlinear *vocalization*, which, as a system, is far more complete and coherent, still presupposes the Palestinian as a basis."

[4] Revell, "Hebrew Accents and Greek Ekphonetic Neumes," 148–149, and *Biblical Texts with Palestinian Pointing and Their Accents*, xii–xiii.

[5] Revell, "Hebrew Accents and Greek Ekphonetic Neumes," 148, and Yeivin, *Introduction to the Tiberian Masorah*, 166, provide examples (TS 12:197, TS NS 246:22, and P208).

[6] Revell, *Biblical Texts with Palestinian Pointing*, xii.

Appendix B Three Accentuation Systems 145

Palestinian and Tiberian accent systems rarely conflict with each other on most major issues.[7]

Regarding the Babylonian tradition, some traces of accentual development can be observed. In the early period, the early Babylonian accentuation system differs considerably from the Tiberian accentuation system. In the early Babylonian system, for example, the accent marked by a mutilated ש (the Tiberian *Segolta*) appears in both halves of the verse, but *Segolta* is only governed in the domain of *Athnach* in the Tiberian system.[8] As another example, in the early Babylonian system the accent marked by a letter ת (the Tiberian *Tebir*) is the main divider in the domain of another accent ז (the Tiberian *Zaqeph*) and also serves as a final disjunctive (D2f before *Tiphcha* in Tiberian). This can be contrasted with the Tiberian system, in which only the final dividers serve to indicate a final disjunctive.[9] There is other evidence of differences between the early Babylonian and Tiberian accentuation systems. Repetition of the same accent is quite common in the Tiberian system, but very rare in the early Babylonian system.[10] In addition, the early Babylonian system does not have conjunctive accent signs. The biggest difference between these two systems, however, is probably that each verse-half has only one contextual clause in the early Babylonian system.[11]

However, in its later forms the Babylonian accentuation system comes to resemble the Tiberian system more closely. At a later stage, the Babylonian manuscripts present a compound pointing system that adds the Tiberian conjunctive

---

[7] Revell, "The Interpretative Value of the Massoretic Punctuation," 67.

[8] Shoshany, "Babylonian Accentuation System," chapter 2.

[9] Cohen, *The System of Accentuation in the Hebrew Bible*, 39–58.

[10] Shoshany, "Babylonian Accentuation System," chapter 2.

[11] Revell, "Hebrew Accents," 149–151; Shoshany, "תפקידם המקורי של טעמי המקרא," 480. Shoshany states that out of 1,948 case studies, 1,665 cases (85.47%) present identical major divisions in both the Tiberian and the early Babylonian system.

146   *Appendix B Three Accentuation Systems*

Table 13 *Babylonian accents and their Tiberian equivalents*

Accents	Sign	Tiberian equivalent
סוף פסוקא *sop psuqa*	No Sign	*Silluq*
סיחפא *siḥpa*	^ בּ	*Athnach* (over the word)
שׁ *šin*	ע בּ	*Segolta* (mutilated *šin* sign)
ז *zayin*	ז בּ	*Zaqeph* (*Great Zaqeph* and *Little Zaqeph* are identical)
ד *dalet*	ד בּ	*Tiphcha* before *Silluq*
רימיא *rimya*	∨ בּ	*Tiphcha* before *Athnach*
נ *nun*	נ בּ	*Legarmeh*
ני *nun-yod*	ני בּ	*Zarqa*
ת *taw*	ת בּ	*Tebir*
נ–נתויה *nun-neṭuya* "slanted *nun*"	ʹ בּ	Used as transformation of a repeated *Rebia*
ח *ḥet*	ח בּ	*Rebia*
ʹ *yod*	ʹ בּ	*Pashta* or *Yethib*
ט *ṭet*	ט בּ	*Geresh* or *Garshaim*
חצי–ט *ḥaṣi-ṭet* "half *ṭet*"	ˋ בּ	Only appears in the early Babylonian ms. Similar to *Geresh*

Appendix B Three Accentuation Systems 147

signs to the early Babylonian system.[12] As far as accentuation is concerned, the later Babylonian system is far closer to the Tiberian, when compared with the early Babylonian. Table 13 shows the similarities, as well as some of differences, between the Babylonian Hebrew accents and their Tiberian counterparts.[13]

In sum, there is no clear evidence to determine which masoretic tradition is the most ancient of the three even though the Palestinian tradition displays the simplest accentual system. The only thing we can speak to is how the different masoretic traditions influenced each other. Since the Babylonian and Tiberian systems developed separately in two different locales, Tiberian influence on the early Babylonian system was negligible, whereas the later Babylonian system heavily borrowed from the Tiberian accentuation system. Revell rightly states, "the differences between the various Babylonian accent systems could be explained in terms of progressive assimilation to the Tiberian model."[14]

Furthermore, the relationship between the Palestinian and the Tiberian systems differs from the relationship between the Babylonian and the Tiberian systems because both the Palestinian and the Tiberian traditions were included within the streams of a single Western tradition. These two traditions rarely conflicted with each other in major matters, and as a result the differences between the Palestinian and Tiberian accentuation traditions are smaller than the differences between the Babylonian and Tiberian systems.[15]

---

[12] Yeivin, *Introduction to the Tiberian Masorah*, 158–159.

[13] Wickes, *Accentuation of the Twenty-One*, 142–143; Ronit Shoshany, "Biblical Accents: Babylonian," 270, 272–273.

[14] Revell, "Hebrew Accents and Greek Ekphonetic Neumes," 150–151.

[15] Revell, "The Interpretative Value of the Massoretic Punctuation," 67.

Appendix C

The Accents of the "Three Books" in the Tiberian Tradition

As mentioned earlier, there are two sets of accent signs in the Hebrew Bible: (1) the accent signs in the Twenty-One Books (the so-called prose books) and (2) the accent signs in the Three Books (the so-called poetry books). We have focused primarily on the accents of the Twenty-One books throughout this book. Here we will look at the list of accents, the hierarchical relations among them, and the preference of conjunctives in the Three Books.

The Three Books refer to Job (except for the narrative portion of Job 1:1–3:1 and 42:7–17), Proverbs, and Psalms and are also called the "Books of Truth" because of the acronym אֱמֶת ("truth") from the first letters of their Hebrew names, אִיּוֹב (Job), מִשְׁלֵי (Proverbs), and תְּהִלִּים (Psalms).

Several signs used in the Three Books are identical with those in the Twenty-One Books, but their names are different in accordance with their difference in functions.[1] Nevertheless, although the accent signs are different in both systems, both systems are functionally same. Tables 14–18 summarize the basic information regarding the accents of the Three Books, including their names and position, their hierarchical relationships, and the conjunctives preferred by each disjunctive accent.

---

[1] Price, *The Syntax of Masoretic Accents in the Hebrew Bible*, 161.

Table 14 *Disjunctive accents in the Three Books*

Name	Accent position	Remarks	Meaning
Silluq	דָּבָר	–	"separation"
Ole-WeYored	דָּבָר	–	"up and down"
Athnach	דָּבָר	–	"cause to rest"
Great Rebia	דָּבָר	–	"big resting"
Rebia Mugrash	דָּבָר	Prepositive	uncertain
Great Shalsheleth	דָּבָר	–	"big triplet"
Sinnor	דָּבָר	Postpositive	"canal"
Little Rebia	דָּבָר	Always right before *Ole-WeYored*	"small resting"
Dechi	דָּבָר	Prepositive	"thrust back"
Pazer	דָּבָר	–	"scattering"
Mahpak Legarmeh	דָּבָר	–	–
Azla Legarmeh	דָּבָר	–	–

Table 15 *Conjunctive accents in the Three Books*

Name	Accent Position	Remarks	Meaning
Munach	דָּבָר	–	"sustained"
Mereka	דָּבָר	–	"prolonged"
Illuy	דָּבָר	–	"above"
Tarcha	דָּבָר	Same shape with *Tiphcha*	"slow"
Galgal	דָּבָר	–	"rolling over"
Mahpak	דָּבָר	–	"inverted"
Azla (or *Qadma*)	דָּבָר	–	"proceeding"
Little Shalsheleth	דָּדָר	–	"small triplet"
Sinnorit Mereka	דָּבָר	–	–
Sinnorit Mahpak	דָּבָר	–	–

Appendix C The Accents of the "Three Books"   151

Table 16 *Hierarchy among the disjunctives in the Three Books*[a]

| Hierarchy | Disjunctive accents | Defined subordinates | |
		Near	Remote
I	*Silluq*	*Rebia Mugrash*	*Athnach/Ole-WeYored*
(D0)			
II	*Rebia Mugrash*	*Dechi*	*Great Rebia*
(D1)	*Athnach*	*Dechi*	*Great Rebia*
	Old-WeYored	*Sinnor*	*Great Rebia*
III	*Dechi*	*Legarmeh*	*Pazer*
(D2)	*Sinnor*	*Legarmeh*	*Pazer*
	Great Rebia	*Legarmeh*	*Pazer*
IV	*Pazer*	*Legarmeh*	Empty
(D3)	*Legarmeh*	*Legarmeh*	Empty

[a] Price, *The Syntax of Masoretic Accents in the Hebrew Bible*, 167

Table 17 *Substitute disjunctives for regular disjunctives in the Three Books*[a]

Regular disjunctives	Substitute disjunctives
Rebia Mugrash	*Great Shalsheleth*
Sinnor	*Little Rebia*

[a] Price, *The Syntax of Masoretic Accents in the Hebrew Bible*, 168.

Having summarized the most important information regarding the accents of the Three Books, let us analyze some verses from the Three Books in light of the general framework for understanding the accents presented in this book. Psalm 1:1–6 presents a good case study. We begin with v. 1:

152 Appendix C The Accents of the "Three Books"

Table 18 *Preference of conjunctives in the Three Books*[a]

Disjunctives	Numbers of permitted conjunctives	Preference of conjunctives
Silluq	0–1	Munach or Mereka (after Rebia Mugrash)/ Illuy (after Mahpak-Legarmeh)
Rebia Mugrash	0–1	Mereka
Great Shalsheleth	0–1	Mereka
Athnach	0–1	Munach (after Dechi or Virtual Dechi)/ Mereka (after any other disjunctives)
Ole-WeYored	0–1	Either Galgal or Mahpak after Sinnor
Dechi	0–1	Munach
Sinnor	0–1	Either Munach or Mereka under certain conditions
Little Rebia	0–1	Mereka
Great Rebia	0–1	Either Illuy or Mahpak or Sinnorit-Mahpak under certain conditions
Pazer	0–1	Galgal
Azla Legarmeh	0–1	Either Illuy or Mahpak or Sinnorit-Mahpak under certain conditions
Mahpak Legarmeh	None	–

[a] Price, *The Syntax of Masoretic Accents in the Hebrew Bible*, 169.

אַשְׁרֵי־הָאִישׁ	אֲשֶׁר |	לֹא	הָלַךְ	בַּעֲצַת רְשָׁעִים /
Great Rebia	Mahpak Legarmeh	Mereka	Sinnor	Ole-WeYored Galgal
D2	D3		D2	D1

וּבְדֶרֶךְ	חַטָּאִים	לֹא	עָמָד //
Munach	Dechi	Mereka	Athnach
	D2		D1

וּבְמוֹשַׁב	לֵצִים	לֹא	יָשָׁב:
Mereka	Rebia Mugrash	Munach	Silluq
	D1		D0

Appendix C The Accents of the "Three Books"

Blessed is the man who does not walk in the counsel of the wicked /
or stand in the way of sinners //
or sit in the seat of mockers.

Three comments are in order as we consider the diagram of Psalm 1:1. First, the methods for dividing a verse in the Three Books are not different from those in the Twenty-One Books. Like the Twenty-One Books, the Three Books also exhibit hierarchical relationship among disjunctives (see Table 16) and final disjunctives. This means that we can apply the same steps for dividing a verse discussed earlier (see Section 2.2) to any verse in the Three Books. If we were to divide the first line of Psalm 1:1, it would be depicted as follows:

Second, *Athnach* and *Ole-WeYored* usually have equal dividing force in a verse. This means that the majority of poetic lines in the Three Books exhibit a tripartite division rather than a bipartite division as in the Twenty-One Books. Rarely do verses have only *Silluq* without *Athnach* or *Ole-WeYored*, and when they do, the verse is treated as one poetic line.

Third, under the domain of *Athnach*, *Munach* almost always appears after *Dechi*.[2] However, there are exceptions to this general rule. We see this in the second line of Psalm 1:1, in which *Mereka* appears instead of *Munach*.

---

[2] Price, *The Syntax of Masoretic Accents in the Hebrew Bible*, 218.

154   *Appendix C The Accents of the "Three Books"*

Let us move on to the next verse, Psalm 1:2. Notably, this
verse has no *Athnach*:

כִּ֣י אִ֤ם בְּתוֹרַ֣ת יְהוָ֔ה חֶ֫פְצ֥וֹ /
                          Ole-WeYored   *Little*
                                          Rebia

וּבְתוֹרָת֗וֹ יֶהְגֶּ֖ה יוֹמָ֥ם וָלָֽיְלָה׃
Silluq   *Rebia*
                      Mugrash

Indeed, his delight is in the law of the LORD, /
and he meditates on His law always.

As is evident from the diagram above, the signs of *Little
Rebia* and *Great Rebia* are identical. The only way to distinguish
these two accents is to check whether or not the accent in
question functions as the near subordinate segment under
the domain of *Ole-WeYored*. If so, then it is *Little Rebia*, the
substitute for *Sinnor*. In Psalm 1:2, the accent immediately
before *Ole-WeYored* is *Little Rebia*. *Little Rebia* usually serves only
one conjunctive *Mereka*; however, in this case, a *Mahpak* and
another *Mereka* appear on the first two words because they are
monosyllabic particles that should be connected by *Maqqeph*.[3]

Another important observation regarding this verse is that
in the second line, *Rebia Mugrash* is written without the
accompanying *Geresh* sign before *Silluq*. Because it does not
have *Geresh*, it is called "defective *Rebia Mugrash*."[4]

---

[3] Price, *The Syntax of Masoretic Accents in the Hebrew Bible*, 245.
[4] Price, *The Syntax of Masoretic Accents in the Hebrew Bible*, 205.

Appendix C The Accents of the "Three Books"   155

Let us now consider Psalm 1:3:

עַל־פַּלְגֵי מָיִם /   שָׁתוּל   כְּעֵץ   וְהָיָה
Ole-WeYored   *Galgal*   *Sinnor*   *Great Rebia*

לֹא־יִבּוֹל //   וְעָלֵהוּ   בְּעִתּוֹ   יִתֵּן | פִּרְיוֹ   אֲשֶׁר
Athnach   *Virtual Dechi*   *Great Rebia*   *Illuy*   *Azla Legarmeh*   *Mahpak*

יַצְלִיחַ׃   אֲשֶׁר־יַעֲשֶׂה   וְכֹל
Silluq   *Virtual Rebia Mugrash*   *Tarcha*

He will be like a tree planted by streams of water, /
which bears its fruit in its season, and its leaf does not
wither. //
Whatever he will do, he will prosper.

Psalm 1:3 is an interesting verse because it contains several
unique features. First, before *Silluq*, *Munach* appears, but this
is actually a virtual *Rebia Mugrash* because *Rebia Mugrash*
cannot stand on the first word before *Silluq*, if the word with
Silluq is short.[5] So, in this case, *Rebia Mugrash* is transformed
into an appropriate conjunctive, in this case *Munach*.

Second, and similarly, before *Athnach Mereka* appears, but
here we have a virtual *Dechi*. *Dechi* cannot stand on the first
word before *Athnach* when the word with *Athnach* is short.[6]
Therefore, *Dechi* is transformed into a conjunctive, in this
case *Mereka*. The word with *Athnach* (לֹא־יִבּוֹל) is not short
because there are two syllables before the main accent, so
this instance does not present an exception to the usual rule.

Third, as the diagram of Psalm 1:3 depicts, *Ole-WeYored* is
often written defectively in *BHS*. In the first line, the two

---

[5] Price, *The Syntax of Masoretic Accents in the Hebrew Bible*, 209.
[6] Price, *The Syntax of Masoretic Accents in the Hebrew Bible*, 234–236.

156 — *Appendix C The Accents of the "Three Books"*

marks of this accent appear respectively on the last two words, which are in the construct relationship (עַל־פַּלְגֵי מָיִם).

We conclude our brief exploration of the accents of the Three Books by dividing Psalm 1:4–6. These three verses consist of three bicola:

לֹא־כֵן הָרְשָׁעִים //
Athnach

כִּי אִם־כַּמֹּץ אֲשֶׁר־תִּדְּפֶנּוּ רוּחַ:
Silluq   *Rebia Mugrash*

The wicked are not so, //
they are indeed like chaff which the wind drives away.

עַל־כֵּן | לֹא־יָקֻמוּ רְשָׁעִים בַּמִּשְׁפָּט //
Athnach   *Dechi*   *Mahpak Legarmeh*

וְחַטָּאִים בַּעֲדַת צַדִּיקִים:
Silluq   *Rebia Mugrash*

Thus, the wicked will not stand in the judgment, //
nor sinners in the assembly of the righteous.

כִּי־יוֹדֵעַ יְהוָה דֶּרֶךְ צַדִּיקִים //
Athnach   *Dechi*

וְדֶרֶךְ רְשָׁעִים תֹּאבֵד:
Silluq   *Virtual Rebia Mugrash*   *Tarcha*

For the LORD knows the way of the righteous, //
but the way of the wicked will perish.

Appendix D

The Functions of Paseq and *Maqqeph*

D.1 Paseq

Paseq is a unique sign. It does not belong to any accentual system even though some accents such as *Legarmeh* and *Shalsheleth* in the Twenty-One Books and *Great Shalsheleth*, *Azla Legarmeh*, and *Mereka Legarmeh* in the Three Books include the *Paseq* sign as a part of their combined accent markers.

This sign looks like a vertical stroke (|) inserted between two words and is always immediately followed by a disjunctive and immediately preceded by a conjunctive accent. This means that *Paseq* is always located directly between a conjunctive and a disjunctive accent.

The meaning of *Paseq* is literally "separator." So, it serves to distinguish two words for various phonetical, syntactical, exegetical, and theological reasons.[1] We turn now to several examples demonstrating these functions of *Paseq* before explaining how to differentiate between *Legarmeh* and a combined form of *Munach* and *Paseq*.

The most significant function of *Paseq* is to juxtapose two consecutive but different words. A good example of this is found in Deuteronomy 8:15,[2]

---

[1] Kennedy, The Note-line in the Hebrew Scriptures, 34–97.

[2] Himmelfarb, "The Exegetical Role of the *Paseq*," 254.

נָחָשׁ | שָׂרָף

Most translations consider שָׂרָף to be an adjective and read something like "poisonous snakes" (NLT), "venomous snakes" (NIV), or "fiery snakes" (NASB). These translations are viable if the *Paseq* is ignored. When we take the *Paseq* into account in our translation, however, it becomes clear that these two words refer to two, not one, animals: "serpent and fiery snake."[3]

Another example of *Paseq* being used to juxtapose two different words comes from 1 Chronicles 8:38.[4]

עֲזְרִיקָם | בֹּכְרוּ

Without vowels and without *Paseq*, this passage could potentially be translated as "Azrikam, his first born" as the Septuagint reads it. Such a translation could be supported by the next verse, which contains a similar expression, אוּלָם בְּכֹרוֹ ("Ulam, his first born"). However, the existence of *Paseq* in v. 38 helps readers avoid any confusion in how to understand the text, in that it marks the juxtaposition of these two nouns and indicates that they should be taken as two separate persons' names. Thus, the correct translation is "Azrikam, Becheru."

Similarly, in Nehemiah 11:33, we find the listed names of three cities: Hazor, Ramah, and Gittim.[5]

חָצוֹר | רָמָה גִּתָּיִם:

Without *Paseq*, one could translate this passage something like "High Hazor."

---

[3] Notably, Isaiah 14:29 and 30:6 also treat these two animals separately.
[4] Wickes, *Accentuation of the Twenty-One*, 122.
[5] Wickes, *Accentuation of the Twenty-One*, 122.

Appendix D The Functions of Paseq **and Maqqeph**

The second function of *Paseq* is to distinguish between two words. Often the distinction made is a phonetic one. This occurs when a word ends and the next word begins with the same sound or letter, especially if the letter is a liquid consonant (ל, מ, נ) because the liquids tend to assimilate easily to the following consonant. In these instances, *Paseq* provides a pause that prevents assimilation and aids clear pronunciation. Consider the following three examples:[6]

Numbers 32:33 (same letter)

לָהֶם ׀ מֹשֶׁה

Genesis 3:15 (same sound)

וְאֵיבָה ׀ אָשִׁית

1 Chronicles 22:5 (same letter)

לְהַגְדִּיל ׀ לְמַעְלָה

Sometimes *Paseq* is used to distinguish between two words for theological reasons. Within this type of usage, *Paseq* commonly marks a pause before or after God's name, as the following two examples demonstrate.[7]

Exodus 15:18

יְהוָה ׀ יִמְלֹךְ לְעֹלָם וָעֶד:

"The LORD shall reign forever and ever."

Exodus 23:17

יֵרָאֶה כָּל־זְכוּרְךָ אֶל־פְּנֵי הָאָדֹן ׀ יְהוָה:

---

[6] Wickes, *Accentuation of the Twenty-One*, 124.
[7] Wickes, *Accentuation of the Twenty-One*, 126.

Appendix D The Functions of Paseq and Maqqeph

"All your men shall appear before The LORD, Yahweh!"

Yet another reason *Paseq* is used to distinguish between two words is to make a syntactic distinction between אמר and the direct speech that directly follows. This usage is evident in 1 Kings 11:22:[8]

1 Kings 11:22

וַיֹּ֤אמֶר לֹו֙ פַּרְעֹ֔ה

כִּ֠י מָה־אַתָּ֤ה חָסֵר֙ עִמִּ֔י

וְהִנְּךָ֥ מְבַקֵּ֖שׁ לָלֶ֣כֶת אֶל־אַרְצֶ֑ךָ

וַיֹּ֣אמֶר ׀ לֹ֗א כִּ֥י שַׁלֵּ֖חַ תְּשַׁלְּחֵֽנִי׃

Pharaoh said to him,
"But what have you lacked with me?
Behold, you are trying to go back to your land."
And he said, "Absolutely Not! But make sure to send me away."

In the example, the first two words in the first and final lines are phonetically identical, so there is the potential for listeners to become confused and miss the correct sense of the text. However, with *Paseq* providing an emphatic pause, listeners can clearly understand that the text reads לֹא ("Absolutely not!") rather than לֹו ("to him") in the first line.

Finally, in some instances *Paseq* is used to distinguish between two words that are repeated in the same or similar form. In these cases, *Paseq* helps to express an increasing emphasis, as the following two examples demonstrate:

Genesis 17:13[9]

הִמֹּ֧ול ׀ יִמֹּ֛ול

---

[8] Himmelfarb, "The Exegetical Role of the *Paseq*," 250–251.
[9] Wickes, *Accentuation of the Twenty-One*, 123.

Appendix D *The Functions of Paseq* and Maqqeph   161

"He will surely be circumcised"

Number 17:28[10]

כָּל הַקָּרֵב ׀ הַקָּרֵב אֶל־מִשְׁכַּן יְהוָה יָמוּת

"Whoever comes near, surely comes near to the tabernacle of the LORD will die."

Having discussed the basic function of *Paseq*, we need to address one final matter regarding this particular accent: how to distinguish it from the accent *Legarmeh* when it appears in combined form with *Munach*. Several clues enable us to distinguish between the two:[11] (1) if a conjunctive follows *Paseq*, it must be *Legarmeh* because *Paseq* is always immediately followed by a disjunctive and also always immediately preceded by a conjunctive, (2) *Legarmeh* mostly appears before *Rebia*, occasionally before *Pashta*, and rarely before *Geresh*, and (3) since *Legarmeh* is a disjunctive, it governs *Mereka* in first place and *Azla* in second place.

The following verses demonstrate how these three clues can be used to distinguish *Legarmeh* from a combined form of *Munach* and *Paseq*.

Genesis 7:23

וַיִּמַח אֶת־כָּל־הַיְקוּם ׀ אֲשֶׁר ׀ עַל־פְּנֵי הָאֲדָמָה

In this example there are two occurrences of *Paseq* with what initially looks like *Munach*. Because both are under the domain of *Rebia*, the accent accompanying the second occurrence of *Paseq* is *Legarmeh*. The first occurrence of *Paseq* with what looks like *Munach* is preceded by *Geresh*, a disjunctive accent, so this is also *Legarmeh*. It is very rare for *Legarmeh* to be repeated, as is the case here.

---

[10] Cohen, *The System of Accentuation in the Hebrew Bible*, 86.
[11] Price, *The Syntax of Masoretic Accents in the Hebrew Bible*, 122–123.

162 *Appendix D The Functions of Paseq* **and Maqqeph**

Numbers 11:26

וַיִּשָּׁאֲר֣וּ שְׁנֵֽי־אֲנָשִׁ֣ים ׀ בַּֽמַּחֲנֶ֡ה שֵׁ֣ם הָֽאֶחָ֣ד ׀ אֶלְדָּ֡ד

Pazer Paseq Munach Munach Pazer   Paseq Munach   Munach

Like the previous example, there are two occurrences of *Paseq* with what looks like *Munach*. The difference is that the accents are actually *Munach* in this instance, rather than *Legarmeh*. We know this because *Pazer* follows *Paseq* instead of *Rebia, Pashta,* or *Geresh.*

Nehemiah 8:7

וְיֵשׁ֨וּעַ וּבָנִ֜י וְשֵׁרֵֽבְיָ֣ה ׀ יָמִ֣ין עַקּ֗וּב

Pazer   Pazer Paseq Munach   Pazer Pazer

שַׁבְּתַ֣י ׀ הֽוֹדִיָּ֥ה מַעֲשֵׂיָ֥ה

Pazer   Pazer Paseq Munach

This verse presents an unusual combination of accents because there are six *Pazers* and two occurrences of *Paseq* with what looks like *Munach*. Once again, because the accent in question is followed by *Pazer* rather than *Rebia, Pashta,* or *Geresh,* we know that the accent must be *Munach.*

2 Kings 2:12

וְה֣וּא מְצַעֵ֔ק אָבִ֣י ׀ אָבִ֗י

Rebia   Legarmeh Pashta

In this final example, the *Paseq* and what looks like *Munach* are under the domain of *Rebia* and preceded by *Pashta.* Therefore, the accent accompanying *Paseq* must be *Legarmeh* rather than *Munach.*

Appendix D The Functions of Paseq and Maqqeph   163

D.2 Maqqeph

Maqqeph literally means "conjoiner." As such, it serves to cliticize (i.e., attach) a word to what follows in order to avoid main stress crash or reduce the main stress (see Section 6.3). In a sense, the use of *Maqqeph* functions as a kind of simplification process because it eliminates the main stress (es) of clitic word(s). *Maqqeph* can join up to four words (cf. Exodus 22:8), but regardless of the number, it conveys phonological and prosodic changes at the word level.

The conjoining process marked by *Maqqeph* is quite complex, and we cannot always know why it is used. But here are three basic principles that describe the use of *Maqqeph*:

(1) *Maqqeph* is rarely found under the domain of Do level or *Little Zaqeph*. This is because of its prosodic function in speech, which is the same as the simplification process that hardly occurs under the domain of Do level or *Little Zaqeph*. This means *Maqqeph* often appears under the domain of *Geresh*, *Pazer*, and *Telisha*,

(2) The probability that a clitic word will take *Maqqeph* directly depends on its syllable structure. The likelihood of *Maqqeph* occurring progressively decreases according to the following hierarchy: CVC (אֶת, אֶל, פֶּן, בַּת) > CVV (מִי, אוֹ, לֹא, כִּי) > CVVC (שְׂעִיר, בֵּין, אִישׁ) > polysyllabic words (מִבְּבֵי, כַּאֲשֶׁר),

(3) When two or more words are conjoined, the vowel length of clitic words tends to be shortened. Most often, *Segol* replaces *Ṣere* (cf. שֵׁם/שֶׁם־) and *Qameṣ Ḥaṭuph* replaces *Ḥolem* (cf. כֹּל/כָּל־).

Let us consider some passages that illustrate these basic principles for *Maqqeph*:

Leviticus 25:5

אֵת סְפִיחַ קְצִירְךָ לֹא תִקְצוֹר וְאֶת־עִנְּבֵי נְזִירֶךָ לֹא תִבְצֹר

164   *Appendix D The Functions of Paseq* and **Maqqeph**

In this example, the word אֵת joined by *Maqqeph* carries *Segol*, but the word אֵת without *Maqqeph* instead has *Ṣere*. Notably, the word עִנְבֵי is joined to וְאֵת with *Maqqeph* even though עִנְבֵי and נְזִירֶךָ are in construct chain.

2 Chronicles 13:11

$$\text{עֹלֹות בַּבֹּקֶר־בַּבֹּקֶר וּבָעֶרֶב־בָּעֶרֶב וּקְטֹרֶת־סַמִּים}$$
$$\text{וּמַעֲרֶכֶת לֶחֶם}$$

Here, three *Maqqeph*s appear under the domain of *Geresh*. Interestingly, all three clitic words maintain their accents, each of which is replaced by major *Metheg* in an open syllable. As long as the conditions for *Metheg*'s usage are otherwise met, *Metheg* can appear on the clitic word. This is illustrated by the following examples from Exodus 6:6, 1 Kings 1:19, and 1 Chronicles 14:11:

Exodus 6:6 (two syllables before the main stress)

$$\text{לִבְנֵי־יִשְׂרָאֵל}$$

1 Kings 1:19 (minor *Metheg* in a closed syllable)

$$\text{וּמְרִיא־וְצֹאן}$$

1 Chronicles 14:11 (two syllables and a *shewa* before the main stress)

$$\text{בְּבַעַל־פְּרָצִים}$$

Bibliography

Aronoff, M. "Orthography and Linguistic Theory: The Syntactic Basis of Masoretic Hebrew Punctuation." *Language* 61 (1985): 28–72.

Avinum, S. "Syntactic, Logical and Semantic Aspects of Masoretic Accentuation Signs." *Leshonenu* 13 (1989): 157–192.

Barr, James. *Comparative Philology and the Text of the Old Testament.* Oxford: Clarendon Press, 1968.

Bergsträsser, G. *Hebräische Grammatik.* Leipzig: F. C. W. Vogel, 1918–1929.

Blau, Joshua. *A Grammar of Biblical Hebrew.* PLO 12. Wiesbaden: Otto Harrassowitz, 1976.

Bowling, D. L., K. Gill, J. Choi, J. Prinz, and D. Purves. "Major and Minor Music Compared to Excited and Subdued Speech." *Journal of the Acoustical Society of America* 127, no. 1 (2010): 491–503.

Breuer, Mordecai. פיסוק טעמים שבמקרא. Jerusalem: Hahistadrut Hatzionit, 1958.

טעמי המקרא בכ"א ספרים ובספרי אמ"ת. Jerusalem: Mikhlalah, 1982.

Christophe, A., M. Nespor, M. Guasti, and B. V. Ooyen. "Prosodic Structure and Syntactic Acquisition: The Case of the Head-Direction Parameter." *Developmental Science* 6, no. 2 (2003): 211–220.

Churchyard, H. "Topics in Tiberian Hebrew Metrical Phonology and Prosodics." PhD diss., University of Texas at Austin, 1999.

Cohen, D., and D. Weil. "The Original Realization of the Tiberian Masoretic Accents – A Deductive Approach: The Syntactic Function." *Leshonenu* 13, nos. 1–2 (1988–1989): 7–30.

Cohen, M. B. *The System of Accentuation in the Hebrew Bible.* Minneapolis, MN: Milco Press, 1969.

"Masoretic Accents as a Biblical Commentary." *JANES* 4 (1972): 2–11.

Dotan, A. "Prolegomenon-Research in Biblical Accentuation: Backgrounds and Trends." In *Two Treaties on the Accentuation of the Old*

166   *Bibliography*

Testament on Psalms, Proverbs, and Job; on the Twenty-One Prose Books, written by William Wickes, vii–xlvi. New York: Ktav Publishing House, 1970.

"Masorah." In *Encyclopaedia Judaica*. Vol. 13, 2nd ed., edited by Fred Skolnik, 603–656. Detroit, MI: Macmillan Reference USA, 2007.

Dresher, B. E. "The Prosodic Basis of the Tiberian Hebrew System of Accents." *Language* 70 (1994): 1–52.

"Between Music and Speech: The Relationship between Gregorian and Hebrew Chant." *Toronto Working Papers in Linguistics* 27 (2008): 43–58.

"The Word in Tiberian Hebrew." In *The Nature of the Word: Essays in Honor of Paul Kiparsky*, edited by Kristin Hanson, and Sharon Inkelas, 95–111. Cambridge, MA: MIT Press, 2009.

"Stress Assignment in Tiberian Hebrew." In *Contemporary Views on Architecture and Representations in Phonology*, edited by Eric Raimy, and Charles E. Cairns, 213–225. Cambridge, MA: MIT Press, 2009.

Freedman, David Noel, and M. B. Cohen. "The Masoretes as Exegetes: Selected Examples." In *1972 and 1973 Proceedings IOMS, SBLMS 1*, edited by Harry M. Orlinsky, 35–46. Missoula, MT: University of Montana, 1974.

Gee, J. P., and F. Grosjean. "Performance Structures: A Psycholinguistic and Linguistic Appraisal." *Cognitive Psychology* 15 (1983): 411–458.

Gesenius, W., E. Kautzsch, and A. E. Cowley. *Gesenius' Hebrew Grammar*. Oxford: Clarendon Press, 1910.

Gibson, J. C. L. "Stress and Vocalic Change in Hebrew: A Diachronic Study." *Journal of Linguistics* 2 (1966): 35–56.

Ginsburg, C. D. *Introduction to the Massoretico-Critical Edition of the Hebrew Bible with Prolegomenon by Harry Orlinsky*. New York: Ktav Publishing House, 1966.

Goerwitz, Richard L. "Tiberian Hebrew Pausal Forms." PhD diss., University of Chicago, 1993.

Goshen-Gottstein, M. "The Rise of the Tiberian Bible Text." In *Biblical and Other Studies*, edited by A. Altmann, 79–121. Cambridge, MA: Harvard University Press, 1963.

Grosjean, F., L. Grosjean, and A. Deschamps. "Analyse contrastive des variables temporelles de l'anglais et du francais: Vitesse de parole et variables composantes, phénomènes d'hésitation." *Phonetica* 31 (1975): 144–184.

Grosjean, F., L. Grosjean, and H. Lane. "The Patterns of Silence: Performance Structures in Sentence Production." *Cognitive Psychology* 11 (1979): 58–81.

Bibliography

167

Harris, Zellig S. *Development of the Canaanite Dialects: An Investigation of Linguistic History.* AO 16. New Haven, CT: American Oriental Society, 1939. Reprint, New York: Kraus Reprint Corp., 1967.

Hayes, Bruce. "A Grid-Based Theory of English Meter." *Linguistic Inquiry* 14, no. 3 (1983): 357–393.

——. *A Metrical Theory of Stress Rules.* ODL. New York: Garland Publishing, 1985.

——. "The Prosodic Hierarchy in Meter." In *Phonetics and Phonology.* Vol. 1: Rhythm and Meter, edited by Paul Kiparsky, and Gilbert Youmans, 201–260. San Diego, CA: Academic Press, 1989.

Herzog, A. "Masoretic Accents (Musical Rendition)." In *Encyclopaedia Judaica.* Vol. 11, 2nd ed., edited by Fred Skolnik, 656–664. Jerusalem: Keter Publishing House, 2007.

Himmelfarb, Lea. "The Exegetical Role of the *Paseq.*" *Sefarad* 58, no. 2 (1998): 243–260.

Hoop, Raymond de. "The Colometry of Hebrew Verse and the Masoretic Accents: Evaluation of Recent Approach (Part II)." *JNSL* 26, no. 2 (2000): 65–100.

——. "Stress and Syntax; Music and Meaning: The Purpose of Function of the Masoretic Accentuation System." *JNSL* 34, no. 2 (2008): 99–121.

Jacobson, Joshua R. *Chanting the Hebrew Bible: The Art of Cantillation.* 2nd & expanded ed. Philadelphia: Jewish Publication Society, 2017.

Janis, Norman. "A Grammar of the Biblical Accents." PhD diss., Harvard University, 1987.

Kahle, P. E. *The Cairo Geniza.* 2nd ed. Oxford: Basil Blackwell, 1959.

Keller, B. Zellner. "Revisiting the Status of Speech Rhythm." In *Proceedings of the Speech Prosody 2002 Conference,* edited by Bernard Bel, and Isabelle Marlien, 727–730. Aix-en-Provence, France, April 11–13, 2002.

Kennedy, James. *The Note-line in the Hebrew Scriptures: Commonly Called Pāsēq, Or Pěsîq.* Edinburgh: T&T Clark, 1903.

Khan, Geoffrey. *A Short Introduction to the Tiberian Masoretic Bible and Its Reading Tradition.* 2nd ed. Piscataway, NJ: Gorgias Press, 2013.

Kiparsky, Paul. "Metrical Structure Assignment Is Cyclic." *Linguistic Inquiry* 10, no. 3 (1979): 421–441.

Kogut, Simcha. "התייחסותה המפורשת של פרשנות המקרא המסורתית לשאלת המחויבות לטעי המקרא והרקע למחוייבות זו." In *"Sha'arei Talmon": Studies in the Bible, Qumran and the Ancient Near East Presented to Shemaryahu Talmon,* edited by M. A. Fishbane, E. Tov, and W. W. Fields, 153–165. Winona Lake, IN: Eisenbrauns, 1992.

——. המקרא בין טעמים לפרשנות: בחינה לשונית ועניינית של זיקות ומחלוקות בין פרשנות הטעמים לפרשנות המסורתית. Jerusalem: Magnes Press, 1994.

168   *Bibliography*

Kutscher, E. Y. "Contemporary Studies in North-western Semitic." *JSS* 10 (1965): 21–51.

Lee, S. *A Grammar of the Hebrew Language, Comprised in a Series of Lectures.* 2nd ed. London: James Duncan, 1832. Reprint, Charleston, SC: BiblioBazaar, 2008.

Morag, S. "מפעלם של ראשונים: על דרכם של חכמי המסורה ועל מונחים ארמיים שטבעו." *Leshonenu* 38 (1974): 49–77.

Nespor, Marian, and Irene Vogel. *Prosodic Phonology.* SGG 28. Berlin: Mouton de Gruyter, 2007.

Park, Sung Jin. "'Pointing to the Accents in the Scroll': The Functional Development of the Masoretic Accents in the Hebrew Bible." *HS* 55 (2014): 73–88.

    Typology in Biblical Hebrew Meter: A Generative Metrical Approach. Lewiston, NY: Edwin Mellen, 2017.

    "The Validity of the Phonetic Value Changes of *Shewa* in Various Tiberian Accentual Contexts." *HS* 60 (2019): 333–355.

Patel, A. *Music, Language, and the Brain.* Oxford: Oxford University Press, 2008.

Poebel, A. "The Antepenult Stressing of Old Hebrew and Its Influence on the Shaping of the Vowels." *AJSL* 56, no. 3 (1939): 225–230.

    "Penult Stressing Replacing Ultimate Stressing in Pre-Exilic Hebrew." *AJSL* 56, no. 4 (1939): 384–387.

Price, J. D. *The Syntax of Masoretic Accents in the Hebrew Bible.* SBEC 27. Lewiston, NY: Edwin Mellen, 1990.

    "Exegesis and Pausal Forms with Non-Pausal Accents in the Hebrew Bible." Paper Presented at the Southeastern Regional Meeting of the ETS, March 18, 2006. http://www.jamesdprice.com/images/Pausal_Forms_ETS_paper.pdf.

Prince, Alan S. "The Phonology and Morphology of Tiberian Hebrew." PhD diss., MIT, 1975.

    "Relating to the Grid." *Linguistic Inquiry* 14, no. 1 (1983): 19–100.

Revell, E. J. "The Oldest Evidence for the Hebrew Accent System." *BJRL* 54 (1971/72): 214–222.

    "Biblical Punctuation and Chant in the Second Temple Period." *JSJ* 7 (1976): 181–198.

    Biblical Texts with Palestinian Pointing and Their Accents. SBLMS 4. Missoula, MT: Scholars Press, 1977.

    "Hebrew Accents and Greek Ekphonetic Neumes." In *Studies in Eastern Chant IV,* edited by Miloš Velimirović, 140–170. London: Oxford University Press, 1979.

    "Pausal Forms in Biblical Hebrew: Their Function, Origin and Significance." *JSS* 25 (1980): 165–179.

Bibliography 169

"Pausal Forms and the Structure of Biblical Poetry." *VT* 31 (1981): 186–199.

"*Nesiga* and the History of the Masorah." In *Estudios Masoretico: V Congreso de la IOMS: Dedicados a Harry M. Orlinsky.* Textos y Estudio Cardenal Cisneros 33, edited by Emilia Fernandez Tejero, 37–48. Madrid: C.S.I.C., 1983.

Nesiga (Retraction of Word stress) in Tiberian Hebrew. Textos y Estudios Cardenal Cisneros 39. Madrid: Instituto de Filología, 1987.

"Masoretic Accent." In *ABD.* Vol. 4, edited by D. N. Freedman, 594–596. New York: Doubleday, 1992.

"The Interpretative Value of the Masoretic Punctuation." In *The Middle Age. From the Beginnings to the Middle Ages (Until 1300), Part 1. Hebrew Bible/Old Testament: The History of Its Interpretation,* Vol. 1, edited by Magne Sæbø, 64–73. Gottingen: Vandenhoeck & Ruprecht, 2000.

Ross, D., J. Choi, and D. Purves. "Musical Intervals in Speech." *Proceedings of the National Academy of Sciences of the United States of America* 104, no. 23 (2007): 9852–9857.

Selkirk, Elisabeth O. *Phonology and Syntax: The Relation between Sound and Structure.* Cambridge, MA: MIT Press, 1984.

Shoshany, Ronit. "Babylonian Accentuation System: Rules of Division and Accentuation, Stages of Development, and Relationship to the Tiberian System." PhD. diss., Tel-Aviv University, 2003.

"תפקידם המקורי של טעמי המקרא." In משאת אהרן: מחקרים בלשון מוגשים לאהרן דותן, edited by Moshe Ben-Asher, and Chaim E. Cohen, 469–486. Jerusalem: Mosad Bialik, 2009.

"Biblical Accents: Babylonian." In *Encyclopedia of Hebrew Language and Linguistics,* Vol. I: A–F, edited by Geoffrey Khan, 268–275. Leiden: Brill, 2013.

Tov, E. *Textual Criticism of the Hebrew Bible.* 2nd ed. Minneapolis, MN: Fortress Press, 2001.

Treitler, Leo. "Reading and Singing: On the Genesis of Occidental Music-Writing." *Early Music History: Studies in Medieval and Early Modern Music* 4 (1984): 135–208.

Waltke, B. K., and M. O'Connor, *An Introduction to Biblical Hebrew Syntax.* Winona Lake, IN: Eisenbrauns, 1990.

Weil, Daniel M. *The Masoretic Chant of the Bible.* Jerusalem: Rubin Mass Ltd. Publishers, 1985.

Weisberg, D. B. "The Rare Accents of the Twenty-One Books." *JQR* 56, no. 4 (1966): 314–336; 57, no. 1 (1967): 57–70; 57, no. 3 (1967): 227–238.

170   *Bibliography*

Werner, E. *The Sacred Bridge: The Interdependence of Liturgy and Music in Synagogue and Church during the First Millennium.* New York: Columbia University Press, 1959.

Wickes, W. *A Treatise on the Accentuation of the Three So-Called Poetical Books of the Old Testament: Psalms, Proverbs, and Job.* London: Oxford University Press, 1881.

  A Treatise on the Accentuation of the Twenty-One So-Called Prose Books of the Old Testament. London: Oxford University Press, 1887.

Yeivin, I. *Introduction to the Tiberian Masorah.* Translated and edited by E. J. Revell. SBLMS 5. Missoula, MT: Scholars Press, 1980.

Subject Index

accent, *1–3, 5–9, 10–20, 27–28, 32–33, 38–42,* 46, *49–50,* 53, 55, *58–59, 61–63,* 65, *67–69, 73–75,* 80, 82, 85, *88–89,* 91, *93–98,* 112, *114–121, 125–126,* 131, *135–139, 141–147,* 151, 155, 157, *161–162,* 164
  accentual divisions, 93–94, 99, 102, 111, 115, 118, 120–121, 125, 129, 131
  conjunctive, 2, 4–8, 11, 15, 17–18, 20, 42, 53–55, 58, 60–61, 63–64, 67–69, 73–76, 78, 80–83, 85, 88, 91, 95–98, 100–101, 120, 129, 137, 139, 143, 145, 149, 154–155, 157, 161
    preference, 53
  disjunctive, 2–3, 5–8, 10–20, 23, 25, 41–42, 46, 49, 53, 56, 67, 69, 73, 75–76, 79–82, 85, 88, 91, 93–95, 98–101, 108–109, 112, 115, 120–121, 129–130, 137, 140, 145, 149, 151, 153, 157, 161
    final disjunctive, 18
    near disjunctives, 19
    regular disjunctives, 12
    remote disjunctives, 19
    substitute disjunctives, 12
  domain, 11, 13–20, 23–30, 32, 34, 36–41, 43, 45–46, 49, 68, 74, 76–81, 108, 110, 129, 145, 153, 161–162, 164
  rare accent, 32
  secondary accent, 7, 27–28, 53, 65, 69, 95
  substitution, 23–24, 26, 29, 32–33, 35, 44, 46–47, 49, 73

accent rules
  dichotomy, 10, 14, 16–17, 20, 33, 50, 84, 114, 137
  division, 14–15, 73–74, 81–85, 88, 93, 99–101, 110, 112, 129, 138, 153
  hierarchy, 10–11, 13, 18, 20, 34, 50, 96, 103–104, 108, 111, 113, 163
  simplification, 74–75, 77–79, 81, 85, 88–89, 129, 163
accentual position
  postpositive, 3–4, 150
  prepositive, 3, 150
accentuation system, 1, 10, 12, 69, 94, 96, 111, *133–134,* 136, *139–141,* 143, 145
  Babylonian, 2, 135, 140, 143, 145, 147
  Palestinian, 2
  Tiberian, 1–2, 4, 12, 23, 26, 60, 62, 65, 68, 74, 81, 86, 94, 97, 103, 107, 111, 113, 115, 133–137, 139–141, 143–145, 147
Athnach, 3–4, 7, 11, *15–17,* 19, 23, *25–28,* 30, 49, *53–54,* 69, 82, 101, 109, 115, 119, *121–122,* 124, 127, 139, *145–146, 150–153*
Azla, 4–5, 27, 43, 49, 53, 59, 61, *63–64, 78–79,* 150, 152, 157, 161

biblical Hebrew poetry
  binary branching system, 14
  parallelism, 14, 112, 115, 118
Books of Truth. See The Three Books
Breuer, Mordecai, 14

cantillation, 12, 93, 99, *136–137,* 142
Cohen, Miles, 5, 14, 18, 27, 29, 31, 39, 42, 46, *73–74,* 81, 98, 119, 121, 145, 161

171

Subject Index

construct chain, 97–98, 100, 120–121,
164

Dagesh euphonicum, 97
Darga, 42, 53, 56, 59, 61, 100
Dechi, 150–153
   virtual Dechi, 152
Deḥiq. See Dagesh euphonicum
diagramming, 10, 14, 20, 107
Dresher, B. E., 26, 74, 81, 94, 103,
   107–109, 113, 133, 139

exegesis, 116, 120, 131

Galgal, 4, 54–55, 150, 152
Garshaim, 3, 11–13, 24, 39–40, 42–43,
   45–46, 48–49, 53, 78–79, 146
Gaʿya. See Metheg
gemination, 96–97
Geresh, 3, 5, 11–12, 15, 19, 25, 30, 35, 37,
   39–40, 42–43, 45–46, 48–49, 54,
   63–64, 68, 78–79, 102, 146, 154,
   161–162, 164

Haggadic tradition, 12
hierarchy level
   D0, 14–17, 19–20, 23–28, 30, 50, 52,
      75, 81–82, 84–85, 107–110, 112,
      151, 163
   D1, 15–17, 20, 23, 25–27, 29–30, 33,
      36–37, 39, 49–51, 75–77, 81–82,
      84, 88, 90–91, 98, 109–110, 151
   D2, 15–17, 19, 24–25, 27–28, 30,
      35–42, 45–46, 49–52, 73, 76–78,
      83, 110, 151
   D3, 14–17, 20, 24–25, 30, 35, 37,
      40–43, 45–51, 75, 77, 79–80, 91,
      129, 151

Illuy, 150, 152

Jewish homiletical interpretation. See
   Haggadic tradition

Legarmeh, 3, 6, 37, 40, 53, 58, 76, 146,
   150–152
   Azla Legarmeh, 154
   Mahpak Legarmeh, 150

Mahpak, 4–6, 42, 54, 58, 65, 68, 150, 152,
   154
Maqqeph, 39, 46, 49, 61, 65–66, 77, 81,
   86, 94–97, 101, 154, 157, 163

Masoretes, 1, 135, 137, 141
Mayela, 7, 65, 69
melodic tone, 12, 38
Mereka
   Double Mereka, 4–5, 42, 53–54, 56,
      58–63, 65, 67, 77, 82–83, 117,
      151–155, 157, 161
meter
   iambic, 73–74
Metheg, 7, 27, 61–62, 65–68, 81, 164
   major Metheg, 65, 68
   minor Metheg, 65–68
   musical Metheg, 65
   phonetic Metheg, 65
   shewa Metheg, 65–66
Munach, 4–5, 7, 27–28, 40, 42, 44,
   53–55, 57–59, 61, 63–65, 76, 79,
   82, 98, 137, 150, 152–153, 155,
   157, 161–162
music
   cantillation, 12, 93, 99, 136–137, 142
   neumes, musical, 23, 31, 33, 141
   notation, musical, 93, 133, 136,
      140–142
   pausal duration, 112, 115, 139

narrative, biblical, 116, 125, 131
Nesiga rule. See stress crash
Nun–neṭuya, 146

Ole–WeYored, 150–153, 155

Paseq, 6, 33, 40, 59, 61, 76, 157–164
Pashta, 3, 5, 11, 13, 15–17, 19, 25, 35–42,
   45–46, 49, 54, 58–59, 68, 75, 77,
   98, 110, 146, 161–162
Pazer
   Great Pazer, 3, 11–13, 35, 42–43,
      46–47, 49, 54–55, 57, 79–80, 141,
      150–152, 162
performance structure, 93, 112–113, 116
phrase
   intonational phrase, 103–104, 106,
      108, 110–111
   phonological phrase, 103
Price, James, 11, 13, 19, 33, 42–43, 46–47,
   53, 101, 109, 137–138, 149,
   161
prosody
   prosodic analysis, 93, 103, 112
   prosodic constituents, 103
   prosodic division, 103–104, 115–116
   prosodic representation, 100, 112

Subject Index

173

prosodic structure, 94, 99, 103–104, 106–107, 112–113, 115, 120, 125
prosodic theory, 103

Rebia, 3, 5, 11, 13, 15, 24, 30, 35, 37, *39–41*, 43, *45–46*, 49, 54, 56, *75–76, 78–79*, 83, 109, 115, *129–130*, 137, 146, *151–152*, 154, *161–162*
  Great Rebia, 150–152, 154
  Little Rebia, 151
  Rebia Mugrash, 151, 154
  virtual Rebia Mugrash, 155
Revell, E., 145, 147
Rimya, 146

sandhi. See spirantization
Segolta, 3, 5, 11, 13, 15, 19, 24, 26, *29–30*, *32–33*, 36, 41, 49, 76, 83, 109, 115, 130, 135, *145–146*
Selkirk, E. O., 104, 108
Shalsheleth, 3, 6, *12–13*, 26, 29, *32–34*, *48–49*, 54, 141, 150, 157
  Great Shasheleth, 152
  Little Shalsheleth, 150
Sihpa, 146
Silluq, *3–5*, 7, 11, *15–17*, 19, *23–25*, 27, 29, *53–54*, 56, 67, 69, *81–82*, 109, 115, 125, *150–154*, 156
Sinnor, *150–151*, 154
Sinnorit
  Sinnorit Mahpak, 150
  Sinnorit Mereka, 150
Sop psuqa, 146
Soph Pasuq, *3–5*, *11–12*, 14, 23
speech perception. See utterance
spirantization rule, 73, 85, 88, *96–97*
stress, 2, 26, 37, 40, 64, 66, 73, *78–79*, *84–86*, 89, *95–96, 98–99*, 103, *134–136*, 144, *163–164*
  main stress, 37, 85, 95, 164
  penultima, 44, 64
  stress crash, 73, 85–86, 89, 163
  ultima, 40, 44, 46, 49, 64, 78–79
syntax, 11, *93–94, 101–102*, 105, 108, 131
  syntactic analysis, 94, 103

Tarcha, 150
Tebir, 3, 5, 11, *15–17*, 19, 25, *35–36*, *41–42*, 45, *48–49, 59–60, 67–68*, *76–77*, 79, 146
Telisha
  Great Telisha, 3, 6, 11–13, 15, 35, 42, 44, 46, 49, 54, 57, 80
  Little Telisha, 4–5, 54, 63–64
The Three Books, 149, 151, 153, *156–157*
The Twenty–One Books, 2, 33, 133, 149, 153
Tiphcha, 3, 5, 7, 11, *15–17*, *24–25*, 27, 30, 49, *53–54*, 56, 67, 69, 76, 81, 83, 99, 110

utterance, *103–104*, 125
  recitation, 94, 115, 139, 142

Wickes, William, 7, 37, 48, *136–137*, 143
word, 2, 5, 12, 15, *17–18*, *26–29*, 32, 36, 38, 40, 43, *45–46*, 49, 61, *63–65*, *67–68*, 73, *75–76, 78–79*, 81, *84–85, 93–95*, 97, 100, 104, *109–110*, 112, 115, 121, 133, 135, 139, 155, 159, *163–164*
  cliticized word, 95
  clitics, 94–95, 104
  grammatical word, 95–96
  long word, 28, 47, 65, 80, 82
  short word, 26
  stem, 96
  vowel–final word, 85, 96–97
  phonological word, 65, 94–97
  word–unit, 12, 29, 34, 36, 38–39, 49

Yethib, 3, 6, 12, 36, 54, 135, 146

Zaqeph
  Great Zaqeph, 3, 11–12, 17–18, 26–27, 34, 49, 54
  Little Zaqeph, 3, 5, 11, 13, 15–19, 24–30, 34, 37, 41, 49, 53, 56, 67–68, 109, 130, 163
Zarqa, 3, 5, 11, 15, 19, 30, 35, *41–42*, 45, 61, 68, 77, 83, 135

Scripture Index

Genesis
1:1, 8
1:2, 35
1:3, 56
1:5, 56
1:11, 57
1:12, 21
1:14, 91
1:20, 26
1:21, 121
1:22, 60
1:28, 30, 62
2:1–4, 9
2:2, 19
2:5, 25
2:6, 65
3:1, 67
3:10, 27
3:12, 56
3:14, 57
3:15, 159
3:17, 36
4:8, 60
4:11, 89
7:23, 161
8:1, 59
9:2, 66
9:24, 67
10:14, 24
11:5, 134
11:9, 20
13:1, 45
13:4, 60
13:14, 59
14:9, 44
14:12, 107
15:17, 134

17:10, 57
17:13, 160
18:7, 102
18:10, 78
18:18, 68
18:31, 59
19:1, 107
19:16, 32–33
20:14, 96
21:14, 50, 129–130
22:10, 101
22:12, 66
22:17, 66
23:10, 107
23:19, 96
24:12, 32–33
24:15, 57
24:27, 45
24:34, 116–117
24:54, 36
25:34, 126
26:6, 24
26:28, 75
27:25, 56
27:37, 39
28:16, 121
28:20, 75
29:6, 134
31:45, 101
35:10, 124
36:21, 61
36:39, 30–31
37:8, 134
38:6, 123
38:6–7, 123
38:13–14, 125
39:8, 32–33

176   *Scripture Index*

Genesis (cont.)
40:16, 56
41:20, 95
42:13, 61
43:7, 64

Exodus
1:1, 4, 24
1:9, 13
5:7, 44
5:15, 96
6:6, 62, 164
7:13, 109
7:19, 64
8:17, 62
10:13, 98
12:4, 36
12:17, 36
12:27, 47
12:29, 41
12:42, 59
12:43, 121
12:45, 67
14:7, 59
14:27, 44, 59
15:18, 159
16:15, 68
16:20, 90
17:6, 78
18:5, 59
18:15, 59
20:9, 62
20:10, 50
21:8, 60
21:13, 59
22:8, 163
23:4, 44
23:17, 159
24:3, 64
24:5, 138
25:35, 43
29:23, 64
30:24, 34
30:32, 28
32:1, 39–40
32:13, 67
32:20, 36
32:27, 70
33:12, 36
34:3, 36
34:18, 36
35:22, 64
35:35, 89
36:6, 63

37:10, 98
37:15, 81

Leviticus
1:5, 65
6:2, 121
6:7, 121
7:20, 40
8:23, 32–33
10:1, 76
10:4, 46
10:12, 69
11:9, 67
12:7, 121
14:51, 68
15:32, 121
18:17, 66
19:36, 87
21:4, 7
23:3, 89
23:27, 79
23:44, 82
25:5, 163
25:46, 68

Numbers
1:18, 110
3:4, 55
4:4, 121
4:14, 57
5:15, 62
7:84, 121
8:11, 89
11:26, 162
13:3, 61
14:40, 42
19:2, 121
21:5, 83
22:20, 63
23:23, 87
25:9, 116
28:20, 27
30:13, 89
31:30, 27
32:33, 159
35:18, 79

Deuteronomy
1:1, 8
2:32, 80
5:7, 67
5:8, 90
7:20, 83
7:26, 66
8:1, 101
8:6, 29

Scripture Index

8:15, 7
9:26, 67
9:28, 34
19:5, 30
22:6, 51
24:22, 27–28
26:2, 61, 91
26:12, 45
29:28, 68
31:22, 66
Joshua
11:8, 63
18:14, 63
Judges
1:1, 22
1:8, 85
2:12, 52
2:20, 37
3:15, 128
3:20, 40
3:21, 128
8:12, 40
16:5, 38
1 Samuel
1:11, 72
2:1, 8
14:42, 17–18
19:12, 127
25:39, 43, 129
30:5, 66
2 Samuel
19:34, 60
20:3, 70
1 Kings
1:19, 62, 164
2:5, 80
6:22, 66
7:48, 21
11:22, 160
14:21, 58
2 Kings
2:12, 162
3:25, 46
10:5, 51, 58
18:21, 97
1 Chronicles
1:50, 30
5:1, 63
8:38, 158
9:44, 59
14:11, 62, 164
21:12, 62
22:5, 159

2 Chronicles
13:11, 164
20:8, 60–61
35:7, 48
Ezra
5:15, 32–33
6:9, 58
Nehemiah
8:7, 162
8:8, 138
11:33, 158
12:44, 63
Esther
8:9, 71
Job
1:1, 133, 149
3:1, 133, 149
3:21, 65
Psalms
1:1, 153
1:1–6, 151
1:2, 154
1:3, 155
1:4–6, 156
Ecclesiastes
1:7, 68
7:10, 68
Isaiah
1:3, 59
1:5, 61
1:6, 21
1:10, 73, 111
5:1, 15–17
5:12, 60
13:8, 32–33
30:10, 59
30:16, 69
34:12, 87
40:3, 116, 118–119
40:13, 98
44:9, 120
53:2, 116, 119
57:8, 66
Jeremiah
2:24, 88
2:31, 69
8:18, 67
11:4, 64
35:15, 57
38:25, 48
41:1, 57
Ezekiel
42:5, 66

Scripture Index

Daniel
6:12, 121, 123
Amos
1:2, 32–33
Jonah
1:2–3, 127
Micah
1:6, 61
John
1:23, 119